CREATING NONGRADED K–3 CLASSROOMS: TEACHERS' STORIES AND LESSONS LEARNED

CORWIN
PRESS

The Corwin Press logo — a raven striding across an open book — represents the happy union of courage and learning. We are a professional-level publisher of books and journals for K-12 educators, and we are committed to creating and providing resources that embody these qualities. Corwin's motto is "Success for All Learners."

CREATING NONGRADED K–3 CLASSROOMS: TEACHERS' STORIES AND LESSONS LEARNED

Ric A. Hovda ▪ Diane W. Kyle ▪ Ellen McIntyre
University of Louisville

CORWIN PRESS, INC.
A Sage Publications Company
Thousand Oaks, California

For information address:

Corwin Press, Inc.
A Sage Publications Company
2455 Teller Road
Thousand Oaks, California 91320
e-mail: order@corwin.sagepub.com

SAGE Publications Ltd.
6 Bonhill Street
London EC2A 4PU
United Kingdom

SAGE Publications India Pvt. Ltd.
M-32 Market
Greater Kailash I
New Delhi 110 048 India

Printed in the United States of America

Library of Congress Cataloging-in-Publication Data

Hovda, Ric A.
    Creating nongraded K–3 classrooms: teacher's stories and lessons learned / Ric A. Hovda, Diane W. Kyle, Ellen McIntyre.
        p.   cm.
    Includes bibliographical references and index.
    ISBN 0–8039–6486–2 (cloth)—ISBN 0–8039–6487–0 (pbk.)
    1. Education, Primary—Kentucky—Case studies.   2. Nongraded schools—Kentucky—Case studies.   3. Group work in education—Kentucky—Case studies.   I. Kyle, Diane Wells.   II. McIntyre, Ellen.   III. Title.   IV. Title: Creating nongraded K–3 classrooms.
LB1511.H84   1996
372.24'1'09769—dc20   94-29654
                                                                                    CIP

This book is printed on acid-free paper.

96 97 98 99 00   10 9 8 7 6 5 4 3 2 1

Design by Joan Gazdik Gillner
Production by Editorial Service and Publications Management
Corwin Press Production Editor: S. Marlene Head

We dedicate this book to the primary teachers of Kentucky and to the children who will become more successful learners because of their teachers' efforts.

In Memorium

To Geraldine Hendricks (1952–1994),
one of Kentucky's outstanding
primary teachers and
a co-author in this book.

TABLE OF CONTENTS

ACKNOWLEDGEMENTS

We would like to thank the teachers, administrators, and parent representatives who have contributed their stories about the experience of educational reform. Their deep commitment to creating excellent and appropriate educational programs for young children is inspirational. We are also grateful to the students in our courses who have offered helpful perspectives and insights and who have asked questions that have challenged our thinking and prompted us to learn more. Angela Burch-Hayden and Libby Clem provided cheerful and prompt support in the preparation of the manuscript. Thank you also to our writers' group—Phyllis Metcalf-Turner, Gina Schack, Lea Smith, and Beth Stroble—for their always-helpful reactions to our writing. To Maureen Awbrey, Kevin McGrew, and Bill Morison, we thank you for your ever-present support and encouragement. And to our former editor, Lloyd Chilton, and our current publisher, Gracia Alkema, a special thank-you for believing that it is important to hear the voices of Kentucky's educators.

CONTRIBUTORS

Karen Adkins teaches a self-contained primary classroom of six- to nine-year-olds at Millard Elementary in Pike County. She is also a thirty-seven-year-old wife, a high school dropout, and the mother of a twenty-year-old son. She has been involved in education since 1984.

Katherine Alexander is a primary teacher at Chenoweth Elementary in Jefferson County. In her fifteen years of teaching, she has taught art, exceptional child education, and fourth grade. She is particularly interested in how children develop as readers and writers. When she is not teaching, she can be found at home with her three cats, reading or writing.

Cheryl Armstrong has taught self-contained special education classes for eleven years. For the past eight years at Paxton Wilt Elementary in Jefferson County, she has taught self-contained multihandicapped students and presently is the collaborating teacher in the nongraded primary program.

Bridget Baker has taught at Ward Chapel Elementary in Bell County as a special educator since 1980. She has worked in the primary program as a team leader, thematic classroom coordinator, and home-base teacher. She served on the Kentucky Department of Education's Primary Task Force and piloted the Kentucky Early Learning Profile. She has received the Outstanding Teacher Award for the Fifth Congressional District and Ashland Oil's Golden Apple Award.

Regina (Jeannie) Bass has been an active member of the Silver Grove School P.T.A. in Campbell County. She has chaired the school's largest fund raiser, served on the site–based council, and been active in many community projects. She has written numerous pieces that have been published in local county publications. She has chosen to focus her career on the development and education of her three children, April, Amanda, and Alanna.

Linda Bibee has taught at Silver Grove School in Campbell County for twenty-two years. She especially enjoys the new freedoms for children in the primary program: kids helping kids and hands-on learning. Linda and her husband, Marc, have two children, Susan, age thirteen, and David, age eight. Linda enjoys reading murder mysteries.

Kathy Birdwhistell team teaches a primary classroom of five- to nine-year-olds with Sheri Cann at Saffell Street School in Anderson County. Kathy has taught for nineteen years.

Sheri Cann team teaches a primary classroom of five- to nine-year-olds with Kathy Birdwhistell at Saffell Street School in Anderson County. Sheri has taught for ten years.

Wendy Combs team teachers a primary classroom of seven-, eight-, and nine-year-olds with Susan Richey at Emma B. Ward Elementary in Anderson County. Wendy has taught for eight years.

Cathy Cool teaches a primary classroom at Cold Spring Elementary in Campbell County. Her particular interests in education include learning styles, diagnostic techniques, and metaphysical philosophy. She has taught for seven years.

Tina Cron teaches a primary classroom with Joy Spears and Donna Stottmann at J. B. Atkinson Elementary in Jefferson County. She is in her fourth year of teaching. She chose a career in teaching after first completing a degree in business. Some of her recent accomplishments include receiving grants to support initiatives in her classroom and presenting with her teaching partners at national conferences. She is currently working on her doctorate in education at the University of Louisville.

Vernell Devine has fourteen years of teaching experience in every grade level except kindergarten. Her most recent experience was in the primary grades. For the past two years, she has been an assistant principal at Mason-Corinth Elementary in Grant County. She continues to stay actively involved in the classroom by teaching classes and working with teachers.

Anne Johnstone Dill has taught for twenty years at a variety of grade levels from primary to high school special education. She and her husband, Gerry, a veterinarian, have a son, Stuart. She has worked with Geraldine Hendricks at Spencer County Elementary in Spencer County for ten years, and they have been partners in their multi-age class for three years.

Sherry Field has taught an integrated primary classroom of seven- and eight-year-olds for two years at Mason-Corinth Elementary in Grant County. She also has four years of experience teaching second grade. She has been involved in thematic teaching and process writing since her first teaching experience.

Wendy Furman is in her second year of teaching and uses thematic and whole language approaches in her primary classroom at Mason-Corinth Elementary in Grant County. She enjoys using the writing process with six-year-olds as well as with ten-year-olds.

Kristin Gregory has twelve years of teaching experience in early primary, most recently at LaGrange Elementary in Oldham County. She has participated in a research study of the nongraded primary and co-authored papers about the findings. Her educational interests are emergent literacy and discovering and developing children's talents and voices.

Diana Heidelberg has been the elementary principal at Silver Grove School in Campbell County for four years. Prior to becoming principal, she taught for sixteen years in special and regular elementary classrooms at Silver Grove School. Primary school and educational reform present daily challenges, which she enjoys tackling. Working with students to become successful is one of her main interests.

Geraldine Hendricks has taught for twenty years, seventeen in first grade and three in multi-age primary with her teaching partner, Anne Dill. They remain committed to providing developmentally appropriate practices to enhance early literacy for children.

Ric A. Hovda is a professor in the Department of Early and Middle Childhood Education at the University of Louisville and director of the Center for the Collaborative Advancement of the Teaching Profession. He teaches graduate courses in literacy, children's literature, and action research. His current research focuses on the development, implementation, and effects of primary programs and interdisciplinary pre-professional and professional development.

Joe Jacovino has been involved in the teaching profession for twenty-five years, the last sixteen as principal at the elementary level. He has taught in several different states and at several different levels, from elementary school to college. He is interested in working with teachers in the areas of student assessment and fostering systemic change. In 1992, he was named the Kentucky Principal of the Year.

Diane W. Kyle is professor and chair of the Department of Early and Middle Childhood Education at the University of Louisville. She teaches graduate courses in elementary curriculum and teachers' action research. She has coauthored *Reflective teaching for student empowerment: Elementary curriculum and methods* with Dorene Ross and Elizabeth Bondy of the University of Florida. Her current research focuses on the development, implementation, and effects of Kentucky's primary program.

Ellen McIntyre is an associate professor in the Department of Early and Middle Childhood Education at the University of Louisville, where she teaches courses on literacy research and instructional methods. Her interests include how children develop as literate individuals in different instructional contexts and in the development, implementation, and effects of nongraded primary programs. She is also co-editor of *Balanced Instruction: Strategies and Skills in Whole Language.*

Gayle Moore has twenty-five years of teaching experience in grades K–8 in Ohio and Kentucky, most recently at LaGrange Elementary in Oldham County. She has participated in a research study of the nongraded primary and co-authored papers about the findings. Her present educational interests include children's academic and social development in nongraded primary classrooms.

Catherine Pillow is a primary teacher at Mason-Corinth Elementary in Grant County. She has been an elementary teacher for sixteen years and has been trained as a K–4 mathematics specialist. She has used thematic teaching effectively for eight years and the writing process with primary-grade children for four years. She considers teamwork and planning with colleagues a major part of a successful primary program.

Phil Poore is a primary teacher at Paxton Wilt Elementary in Jefferson County. He has been a classroom teacher for twelve years, two of those years in special education. He believes in teaching all children, whatever their placement, based on their strengths and needs.

Susan Richey team teaches a primary classroom of seven-, eight-, and nine-year-olds with Wendy Combs at Emma B. Ward Elementary in Anderson County. Susan has taught for twenty years.

Lisa Smith has taught at Ward Chapel Elementary in Bell County since 1982 as a kindergarten, preschool, and primary teacher and as technology lab coordinator. She has been a member of the Kentucky Department of Education's Primary Steering Committee and of the Commonwealth Institute for Teachers and a Kentucky K–4 math specialist. She was selected in 1993 to be a Kentucky Distinguished Educator.

Joy Spears is the collaborating exceptional child educator in a primary classroom with Tina Cron and Donna Stottmann at J. B. Atkinson Elementary in Jefferson County and is in her fourth year of teaching. With her teaching partners, she has presented at the annual meeting of the National Council of Teachers of English, and she is currently involved in studying the primary program. She is married and has one child.

Donna Stottmann teaches a primary classroom with Tina Cron and Joy Spears at J. B. Atkinson Elementary in Jefferson County and has seven years of teaching experience. She and her team members have presented at several national conferences. She has recently participated in the National Writing Project and is currently involved in studying the primary program.

Beverly Wells has spent twenty-one years teaching at all levels from entry through eighth grade. For the past five years, she has taught at Squires Elementary in Fayette County. She believes that the opportunity to teach primary was just the spark she needed at this point in her teaching career.

Vickie Wheatley has had five years of teaching experience at the middle school level and four years at the primary level at LaGrange Elementary in Oldham County. She has completed post-master's coursework. Her present interests include multi-age groupings of five- to nine-year-olds and multiple intelligences.

Anna Yancey has twenty-five years of primary level teaching experience in four schools in Pennsylvania and four schools in Kentucky, most recently at LaGrange Elementary in Oldham County. Her graduate coursework includes an Education Specialist Degree. Her present interests are focused on the Kentucky Education Reform Act primary school program and year-round schooling. Her hobby is writing stories for children.

Reforming the Education of Young Children

BY DIANE W. KYLE,
ELLEN MCINTYRE,
AND RIC A. HOVDA

CHAPTER 1

In this book, we hear the voices of teachers and administrators who, since the fall of 1991, have been engaged in the challenges of educational reform. Specifically, they have responded to a statewide mandate that all elementary schools develop and implement nongraded primary programs for children aged five through nine. Through their accounts, we read detailed examples of such programmatic characteristics as "developmentally appropriate practices," "multi-age/multi-ability grouping," "authentic assessment," "professional teamwork," and "positive parental involvement."

Furthermore, these teachers enable us to understand the personal dimension of professional development and change. Whether at earlier or later stages of their careers, whether more familiar with urban or rural settings, or whether more experienced with kindergartners or third graders, all of these teachers reveal through their writing that who they are as people is intimately connected with who they are as teachers. Their life experiences, beliefs, and attitudes (shared both explicitly and implicitly) provide an important context for understanding their responses to educational change and offer us, as readers, many lessons as we consider our own change efforts.

In the section that follows, we describe the events that led to the development of this book. We then explain the book's organization and content and introduce the teachers whose stories you will soon read.

■ A MANDATE FOR CHANGE

Early childhood educators have reminded us for many years to build school programs on a foundation of what we know about how children grow and learn. They have urged us to remember that play is children's work and to allow time for the socialization that takes place in the block corner, at the art table, and with the props for make-believe. These recommendations reflect the understandings of child development conveyed through the works of such theorists as Piaget (1952; 1955) and Vygotsky (1978; 1986).

More recently, literacy and mathematics specialists have added their voices to this chorus, calling for dramatic changes in the teaching of reading, writing, and mathematics. For example, literacy experts such as Holdaway (1979), Graves (1983), Calkins (1986), Cambourne (1988), Harste (1989), Au (1993), and Goodman, Goodman, and Hood (1989) have suggested that teachers put their basal readers on the shelves and their red correcting pens in their desks. Instead, taking a cue from how children develop oral language, teachers should approach children's learning to read and write in a similarly developmental manner. Children should have many "real" literacy experiences—listening to stories, reading good books, and making early attempts to use writing (even if it's scribbling) to convey meaning.

Operating from a similar perspective, the National Council of Teachers of Mathematics (1989) developed a comprehensive re-design of the standards for teaching mathematics, placing child development at the center of instructional decision making. They suggest that teachers replace the workbooks, worksheets, and drill exercises that have dominated much of mathematics instruction. Instead, they urge teachers to involve children in the use of manipulative materials as a basis for developing conceptual understanding and in activities that demonstrate the application of mathematics to real-life problem solving.

With the suggested innovative instructional practices, the time seems right for more comprehensive reform in how we teach young children. The National Association for the Education of Young Children gave impetus to this effort with their 1988 position statement on developmentally appropriate practices. In this document, the NAEYC outlines the organizational, curricular, and instructional characteristics of programs reflective of children's developmental needs.

In our state of Kentucky in 1990, the education of young children became one of the central features of a comprehensive, systemic reform effort mandated by the Kentucky Education Reform Act, or KERA. *Education Week* heralded the reform as a "landmark $1.2 billion education-improvement package that is one of the most comprehensive ever undertaken by a state" (January 9, 1991, p. 2). One of the most radical components of KERA was the mandate to establish nongraded primary programs in all elementary schools by fall 1993.

The philosophical position statement of the Kentucky primary program (Kentucky Department of Education, 1991) identifies these critical attributes: (1) developmentally appropriate practices as defined by the NAEYC, (2) multi-age/multi-ability groupings, (3) continuous progress, or noncompetitive, individually paced instruction, (4) authentic assessment, (5) qualitative reporting methods, (6) professional teamwork, and (7) positive parent involvement (Appalachian Educational Laboratory, 1991). The statement offers possible strategies for implementing changes consistent with each attribute yet also encourages teachers to interpret and adapt the strategies to their particular classroom settings.

Many teachers took this statement to heart and, before the deadline for full implementation, initiated pilot programs that reflected their own understandings, areas of expertise, resources, and personal styles. The accounts of several of these teachers provide the core of this book. While the critical attributes frame all of their programs, the teachers' descriptions illustrate different starting points in program development and different emphases in program implementation.

■ AN INTRODUCTION TO THE BOOK AND ITS AUTHORS

As faculty members in the Department of Early and Middle Childhood Education, we (the editors) have had many opportunities to be involved in the nongraded primary initiative. We have served as consultants to the Kentucky Department of Education and local school districts, directed and participated in several of the early research studies on the primary program, written about primary program issues and practices, and modified the content of our teacher education courses to include more attention to this topic. We have learned a great deal through all of these experiences, but one realization has continued to surface: *Teachers want to know about and learn from the experiences of other teachers.* In meeting teachers within Kentucky and from the many other states considering similar changes and looking to Kentucky for guidance, we have heard these questions repeatedly:

"Can you tell us where we could visit to see some good primary programs?"

"How are other teachers making so many changes at one time?"

"You travel around a lot. What other kinds of programs have you seen?"

"I know there are meetings of primary program teachers in Kentucky. Is there any way teachers from our state could go? We'd just like a chance to talk to some others who have tried this."

Diane Kyle, Ric Hovda, Ellen McIntyre

This book provides some of those "visits" to primary classrooms and "conversations" with primary teachers. In seeking contributions for the book (through personal contacts and an announcement in a statewide publication), we invited teachers to submit proposals. We asked for brief descriptions of their primary programs and of the information they could share with others. In selecting contributors, we sought to represent different regions of the state, different primary program models, and different types of school districts (urban, suburban, and rural).

We then held two meetings with participants. First, we clarified the book's intent and audience, reviewed the timelines necessary for completing the project, made decisions about both common themes and specific features for each chapter, and organized into teams to read and critique each other's drafts. At the second work session, the writing teams shared suggestions for revisions. As editors, we made further revisions when we received the final drafts; however, in all instances, we attempted to retain the unique voice of the individual writer or writers.

We have organized the descriptions of the primary programs into four sections. (Please note, however, that these sections are not sequential. We encourage readers to make flexible use of the book according to interests and needs.) The first section, "Reform as a Personal Journey," includes three chapters. Katherine Alexander from Chenoweth Elementary reflects on her own childhood experiences and their impact on the primary teacher she has become. Anne Dill and Geraldine Hendricks of Spencer County Elementary share a compelling account of two teachers' struggles and satisfactions in becoming a team. And Cathy Cool from Cold Spring Elementary, in an often humorous account, offers her personal "rules for implementing change."

The second section includes four chapters that address the theme "Understanding Authentic Assessment and Continuous Progress." Four teachers from LaGrange Elementary—Kris Gregory, Gayle Moore, Vickie Wheatley, and Anna Yancey—contribute detailed and useful descriptions of how to document and report students' academic and social development. Following this, Tina Cron, Joy Spears, and Donna Stottmann from Atkinson Elementary offer a vivid portrayal of a team-taught classroom of six- to nine-year-olds, one-third of whom have been designated as having special needs. In their chapter, Phillip Poore and

Cheryl Armstrong of Paxton Wilt Elementary further elaborate on the numerous benefits of an inclusion model and collaborative teaching. And from Saffell Street School, Kathy Birdwhistell, Sheri Cann, Wendy Combs, and Susan Richey share the many insights learned from incorporating a conference approach, children's self-assessment, and portfolios in a primary classroom.

In the third section, the teachers of the three chapters consider the "Challenges of Making Transitions." Bridget Baker and Lisa Smith from Ward Chapel Elementary share the struggles of change that led to their rural school having national prominence. Karen Adkins from Millard Elementary adds another voice to this theme by sharing the challenge of not just making change but sustaining the effort over time. And Beverly Wells of Squires Elementary reflects on the struggle to teach more developmentally and yet confirm that children are learning necessary strategies and skills.

The final section addresses the theme of "Reform as a Shared Endeavor." In the first chapter, Catherine Pillow, Sherry Field, Vernell Devine, and Wendy Furman of Mason-Corinth Elementary reflect on how the joint efforts of teachers and administrators contributed importantly to the development of their program. Joe Jacovino, principal of Camden Station Elementary and Kentucky's 1992 Principal of the Year, shares a similar point of view. Through an account of his school's experiences, he argues that only by bringing in all the stakeholders is systemic change possible. And in the final chapter in this section, Jeannie Bass, Linda Bibee, and Diana Heidelberg of Silver Grove Elementary contribute the perspectives of a teacher, a principal, and a parent to illustrate the development and impact of a nongraded primary program.

We follow the teachers' and principals' stories with a chapter that aims to synthesize several lessons learned across all accounts about creating nongraded primary programs and about professional development needs during such systemic reform initiatives. A concluding chapter offers suggestions on how the book might be used for staff development purposes. Educators wanting to create developmentally appropriate programs for young children can learn so much from those willing to take the risks, invest the time and energy, and face the personal challenges required in "going first." We are grateful to those who have shared their voices.

REFERENCES

Appalachian Educational Laboratory. (1991). AEL Flyer—Ungraded primary programs: *Steps toward developmentally appropriate instruction, a joint study by the Kentucky Education Association and AEL*. ERIC Resource Information Search Package: Ungraded Primary.

Au, K. (1993). *Literacy instruction in multicultural settings*. New York: Harcourt, Brace, Jovanovich.

Calkins, L. (1986). *The art of teaching writing*. Portsmouth, NH: Heinemann.

Cambourne, B. (1988). *The whole story: Natural learning and the acquisition of literacy in the classroom*. Richard Hill, Ontario: Scholastic—TAB.

Commission on Standards for School Mathematics (1989). *Curriculum and evaluation standards for school mathematics*. Reston, VA: National Council of Teachers of Mathematics.

Goodman, K., Goodman, Y., & Hood, W. (1989). *The whole language evaluation book*. Portsmouth, NH: Heinemann.

Graves, D. H. (1983). *Writing: Teachers and children at work*. Portsmouth, NH: Heinemann.

Harste, J. (1989). *New policy guidelines for reading: Connecting research and practice*. Urbana, IL: National Council of Teachers of English.

Holdaway, D. (1979). *The foundations of literacy*. Exeter, NH: Heinemann.

Kentucky Department of Education (1991). *Kentucky's primary school: The wonder years*. Frankfort, KY: Kentucky Department of Education.

National Association for the Education of Young Children (1988). NAEYC position statement on developmentally appropriate practice in the primary grades, serving 5- through 8-year olds. *Young Children, 43*, 64–81.

Piaget, J. (1952). *The origin of intelligence in children*. New York: W. W. Norton.

Piaget, J. (1955). *The language and thought of the child*. New York: World.

Remembering 1990. (1991) *Education Week*, (January 9).

Vygotsky, L.S. (1978). *Mind and society: The development of higher psychological processes*. Cambridge: Harvard University Press.

Vygotsky, L. S. (1986). *Thought and language*. Cambridge: MIT Press.

SECTION 1

REFORM AS A PERSONAL JOURNEY

> I want to tell you a story . . . a story of me as a young girl . . . a story of me as a young woman . . . I want to tell you these stories because they are mine. That young girl and that young woman are vital threads in the woven magic that is my primary program. I want to tell you these stories because I know that to understand my classroom, to understand the teacher I am today, you must understand my journey.
>
> Katherine Alexander
> Chenoweth Elementary School

The stories in this section share how closely the teachers' personal and professional lives interact on their journey toward reform. As they share specific details of their primary programs, they also provide insights into the personal dimensions of professional decision making and the impact this has had on their development.

WE ARE HERE

BY KATHERINE ALEXANDER
Chenoweth Elementary
Jefferson County Public Schools

C H A P T E R

I want to tell you a story of a young girl who loved words, who leaned against her mother's arms and found comfort in the way the words felt as she listened to stories. This child delighted in the sounds of the world around her and, as soon as she was able, claimed the words in books as her own by marking them with the spidery imprint of her name. I also want to tell you the story of a young woman who loved to teach, who found great joy in sharing words and the world with young children, and who wanted to make her classroom a safe place for her students.

I want to tell you these stories because they are mine. That young girl and young woman are vital threads in the woven magic that is my primary program. I want to tell you these stories because I know that to understand my classroom, to understand the teacher I am today, you must understand my journey. It is a journey that began thirty years ago in a very ordinary classroom.

Memories of my first grade classroom flood back to me, washed in sunlight and the warm smell of a new box of Crayolas. I remember the yellow dress that was my favorite that year. I remember my Fred Flintstone lunch box. I remember the fat red pencil I gripped with determination as I worked with the numbers in the workbook on whose cover the green giant stomped. Part of who I am, my intellect and my independence, came to be in that classroom, nurtured by the woman who orchestrated my first educational experience.

But I remember other things as well. I remember that the words I fell in love with as a young girl lost their beauty in school. The words were contorted and jerked as they paraded around the classroom and across our pages. I remember being frequently admonished during reading group as my mind sought escape from these clumsy words. "Stop reading and pay attention! What am I going to do with you?"

I kept these memories in my back pocket for many years, pulling them out only long enough for a promise for when I decided to become a teacher. Soon the memories of my school days were replaced by memories of my early teaching years, stored neatly in boxes on a closet shelf. The boxes are filled with photos of children with gap-toothed grins, pictures drawn with uncertain hands, and notes of love. What is missing from those boxes are the frustrations and the confusions and doubts from those early years, but I remember them, too.

I remember thinking that, armed with teachers manuals and carefully constructed behavioral objectives, I could teach anyone and anything. I remember the confidence draining out of me as I finished lesson after lesson that went "by the book" and noticing that some of the children still did not "get it." I remember my early attempts at watching the children and adjusting the prescribed lessons, afraid that I might be caught. I remember that the more I watched and listened to the children, the more frustrated I became that what I knew about how children learned and how I taught just did not match.

I remember hearing the voice of the young girl shouting, "Stop! Look at what you are doing!"

And what was I doing? Despite all of the promises, despite all of my good intentions, I was teaching exactly as I had been taught. My classroom in those early years was surprisingly similar to the classrooms of my childhood.

What was I doing? I was basing my teaching strategies on the same assumption as in those "You Are Here" signs you see in state parks. Those three little words work wonders if you hit the trail at exactly the right spot. But if you approach the pathway from a different angle, you are out of luck. It is risky business trying this strategy on children. My teacher said, "You Are Here" to me, and she did not alter her teaching when she noticed I was not entirely there. She said, "What am I going to do with you?" instead of "What am I going to do?" I too said, "You Are Here" to my students and kept right on teaching, even when it became clear that some of them were not. It was time for a change.

■ CHANGE THROUGH KID-WATCHING

The change came slowly at first. I read professional books that helped me make the changes, but mostly I watched the children. Little by little, my classroom became a more child-centered place where approximations are expected and praised, where learning is useful, where learning is collaborative, and where learners can take risks.

Walk into my primary program classroom today and you will find a place where children of many ages, backgrounds, and abilities come together to work and grow. It is a classroom organized by workshops that allow children to learn at their own pace. It is a classroom woven together by the threads of belief I have gathered on my journeys as a student and a teacher.

Walk into this Kentucky classroom and meet the children. You will be greeted by Maggie and Stacy, who have a knack for making everyone feel welcome and included right away. You will find Brittany, age seven, with her skill as a diplomat. Suzanne brings her writer's ear and Carole brings her poet's eye to the class. Here is Marcus with his love for the past and Jason and Nathan and Andrew with their unquenchable interest in all things natural. Ben S., age six, and Tim, age nine, both voracious readers, are here.

Here you will find Sam with his unstoppable friendliness and Tristan's wonderful sense of humor. Alex, Ben T., Hunter, and Stuart all have a talent for quiet leadership. Kyle is always willing to take a risk, while Greg prefers a safer road to learning. Lena and Cate have brought their love for the written word and Sara her gift as a dancer.

We are here. Come join us for a day.

Math Workshop
8:45–10:00

> I believe that learning requires practice. Just as an athlete or a musician needs hours of practice to refine his or her skill, so does a child require large blocks of time to practice reading and writing, problem solving, science and social studies.

We begin each day with math workshop. During this time the children work alone, with partners, or in small groups on developmentally appropriate math skills. The workshop begins with a time for practice and application using games and manipulatives. The emphasis here is on understanding the process, not on getting the "right" answer. On a typical day in math workshop, you may see Sam using counters to form two sets and join them together as he practices his addition. Suzanne and Sara use the place value materials to play "Race to a Hundred." You may find Tim at the sink comparing liquid measurements. All the while, the room buzzes with math talk:

"Oh, I get it. They're adding three each time."

"Good for you, Ben! You found a pattern there."

"Maggie, how did you know to multiply there?"

"Ms. Alexander, look. I tried to use a different strategy to regroup in these subtraction problems, but it just didn't work."

Math textbooks on a variety of levels are available for the children's use. With my guidance, the children select a math concept on which to focus for a while and then find a chapter in the text to help them organize their study. Sometimes the children get together to choose their focus concept, since their selection is based on interest and need. As the students are involved in practice and application work, I hold conferences to provide direct instruction to individuals or small groups. Conferences may introduce new concepts, provide remediation, or check progress of individual work. Math workshop concludes with a whole-class activity emphasizing problem solving or "real-life" math skills.

The children keep a weekly math log to record the activities in which they participated and the assignments they completed (see figure 1.1). These logs are sent home every Monday so that the parents can be kept up to date on their child's progress. When the log is returned, it is filed along with work samples and conference notes to be used as a part of the assessment process (see figures 1.2 and 1.3).

FIGURE 1.1

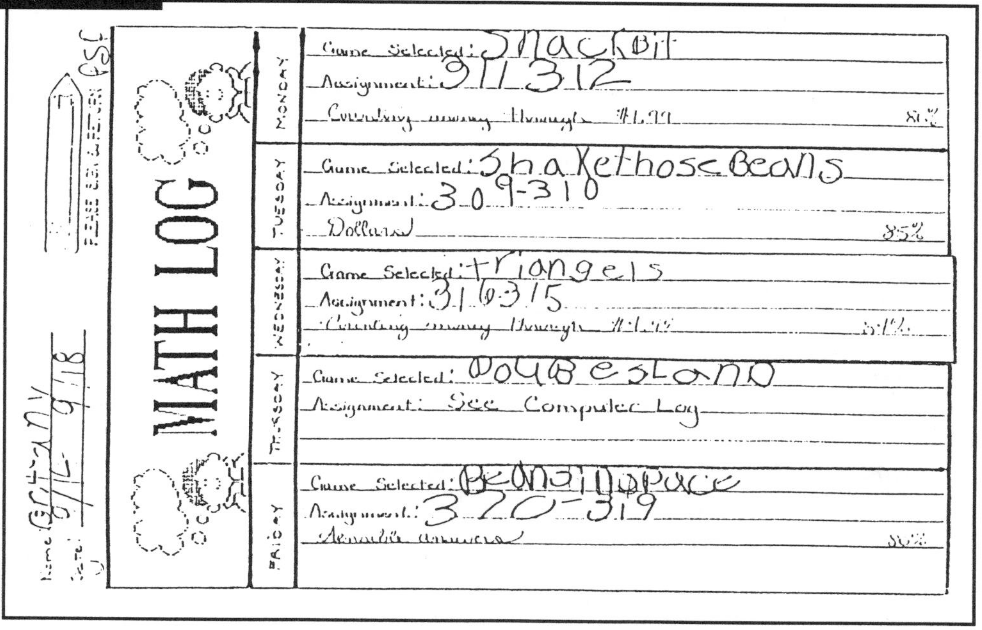

Brittany's Math Log

FIGURE 1.2

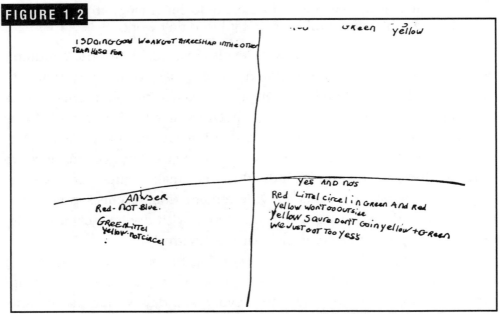

Sample of notes taken by Brittany during a whole class logical reasoning game.

FIGURE 1.3

Brittany 2When I sat 1/28
with B. on Monday (1/25) and
asked her to do some subt./rgrup,
she was able to do it with
little assistance. Today, she was
not able to do so. Confused. I'm
wondering how much problem is
focusing problem.

Conference notes

Unit Study
10:00–11:00

I believe that learning is fun. I love to learn and I try to share that excitement with active lessons as well as with time for quiet reflection.

Science and social studies themes are explored during Unit Study. In this workshop, the content of the subject matter is the focus.

Students read, write, and solve problems, and use and art, music, and drama to explore the concepts related to the theme. The thematic studies last from one to two months and are organized on a three-year cycle.

Unit One: "Home Sweet Home"
    Year 1: Our Bodies
    Year 2: Our Families
    Year 3: Our Homes
Unit Two: "Beyond the Doorstep"
    Year 1: Neighborhoods
    Year 2: Kentucky
    Year 3: Louisville
Unit Three: "New Frontiers"
    Year 1: Coming to America
    Year 2: Moving West
    Year 3: Exploring Space
Unit Four: "Our Physical World"
    Year 1: Music and Sound
    Year 2: Light and Color
    Year 3: Magnets and Electricity
Unit Five: "Changes in Our World"
    Year 1: Food
    Year 2: Clothing
    Year 3: Transportation
Unit Six: "Cycles in Our World"
    Year 1: Rocks
    Year 2: Plants
    Year 3: Animals
Unit Seven: "Regions of Our World"
    Year 1: Oceans
    Year 2: Forests
    Year 3: Deserts

If you drop by during Unit Study, you may find me reading aloud to the children from the diaries of pioneer women to set the stage for our own imaginary journeys west. You may find the children using mirrors and flashlights to discover ways that light behaves. On another day, you may not find us in at all. We're out exploring the neighborhood, seeing how it compares with the ideal neighborhood we designed in the classroom.

The children discover, during Unit Study, that information about the world around us comes from many places. We gather information from books, from art, and from experts. We gather information by manipulating real objects as well.

Sharing the information we gather is a part of Unit Study, too. The children share what they have learned by writing—learning logs, plays, study guides—for other classes. They share information by building models—papier-mâché sod houses or a tropical rain forest that you can actually walk through. It is a time of great excitement. While the children and I explore the themes through active learning in a whole group setting, how the children respond to the learning experience is very individual. Students make frequent entries in learning logs in which they explain and explore what they have learned with words and pictures (see figure 1.4). Parents are kept informed about Unit Study topics through weekly newsletters (see figure 1.5).

FIGURE 1.4

We lernd that sedimentary rod is when sediment gets chiped off of diferent peaces of rock and get conpounded down

Tim, age 9

Sample Learning Log

FIGURE 1.4–CONTINUED

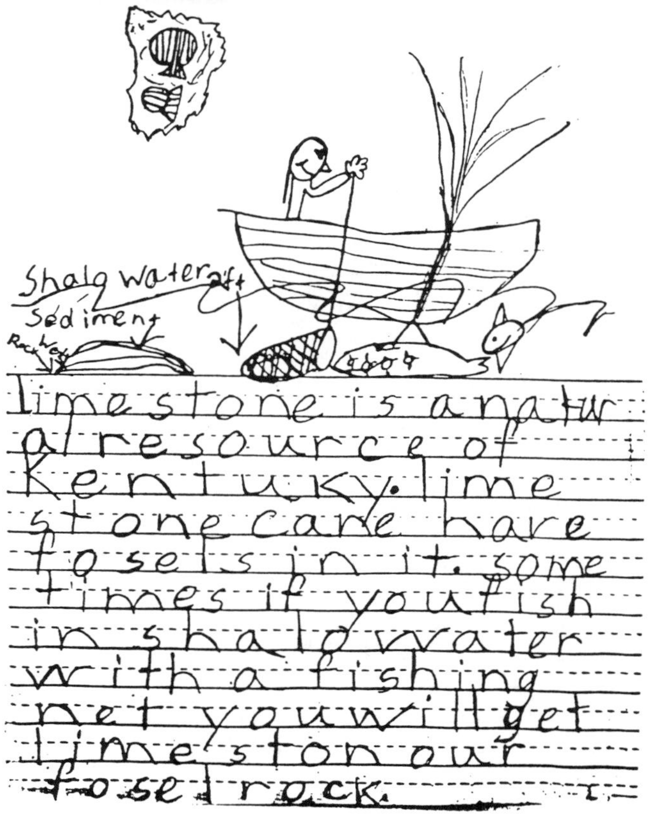

limestone is a natur
al resource of
Kentucky. lime
stone care hare
fosels in it. some
times if you fish
in shalo water
with a fishing
net you will get
limeston our
fosel rock.

Greg, age 6

LIMESTONE IS A FAD rock

Suzanne, age 7

Sample Learning Log

FIGURE 1.5

October 12, 1992

Dear Parents,

There is something reassuring about limestone. I suppose it speaks to that part of me that needs to hear of survival in spite of change. As we sat in the dry creek bed on Wednesday, held in the cupped hands of the hills, I was moved by the constancy of change. Even the air was heavy with the smell of the leaves and branches becoming rich soil.

We spent a few minutes in silence, writing and drawing the plants and animals and rocks around us. It was a nice part of the field trip, I thought. The childen were so excited when we arrived at the creek bed to investigate the limestone and find fossil evidence of Kentucky's geological history that they could hardly contain themselves. We talked before we left about the importance of leaving this environment for future explorers, knowing full well that small bits of rock and fossil would end up in pockets! Other highlights of the trip included passing a limestone quarry in operation off of the expressway and seeing Kentucky's state flower and state tree up close.

In addition to Wednesday's field trip, Unit Study was a flurry of activity. We focused on several of Kentucky's natural resources, including bluegrass, coal and corn. Kentucky is the largest producer of coal in the U.S. We reviewed the story of coal by making layers with our bodies. The bottom layers quickly caught on to the idea of compression! The children learned about the two methods of mining used in Kentucky and discussed the dangers of underground and strip mining to people and to the environment. I told them the story of my grandfather who died in a mining accident in the 1930's. We listened together to Jean Richie's moving ballad "Black Waters" which laments the effects of strip mining in her native Perry County.

While Kentucky is not a large producer of corn compared to other states, corn was certainly an important crop to the early settlers here. We looked at the parts of an ear of corn and discussed how all of the parts were used by the settlers. We're drying the husks and will use them later to create some cornhusk dolls.

We'll continue our investigation of Kentucky's natural resources this week with lessons on sorghum, tobacco and caves. I am still working to complete the Unit Study supplement to the Learning at Home material and hope to have that to you later this week.

Excerpt from weekly parent newsletter

Lunch and Recess
11:00–12:00

> I believe that a classroom should have a sense of community. I want the children in my classroom to know that they are loved and supported. Learning is about taking risks. I try to make the children feel safe about taking those risks.

The children sometimes refer to each other as their daytime family. That sense of community is essential for a successful primary program. After spending three years together, it would be hard not to have that sense of community, but there are some things that a teacher can do to foster such a community. Taking a break together is one small way to promote this camaraderie.

The children and I eat together in the classroom every day. This time away from the hustle and bustle of the school cafeteria allows us time to talk and laugh together and to catch up on the important happenings in our lives. After lunch, the children have a time for freedom from structure. Some choose to organize a game for outside play; some play alone; and others draw, write, or read inside. It is a time for practicing social skills, for learning what it means to be a part of a team, for devising and following rules, for playing, and for sharing.

Enrichment
12:00–12:30

> I believe the arts are basic to a good education.

While using art, music, dance, and drama as tools to explore themes in literature, science, and social studies is important in a primary program, it is also essential to investigate the elements of the arts for their own merit. The arts hold a consistent and prominent place in our daily schedule. During this time, you may find us in the gym making statues with our bodies. You might find us exploring Egyptian design as we make life-size paper sarcophagi. On other days, you may hear us before you see us as the children work in groups to compose musical pieces using rhythm instruments. It is a time filled with much creative energy.

Writing Workshop
12:30–1:30

> I believe that learning requires a wholeness. Nothing can be understood completely by first breaking it down into components so small that they are unrecognizable. Learning to think logically takes place by trying out strategies, not by memorizing facts. Learning about the world around us takes place by observing and experimenting and by physical activity. Learning to write takes place by writing for a real purpose and to a real audience, not by copying someone else's sentences in isolation.

The children often name writing workshop as their favorite time of day. During this workshop, we write, write, rewrite, and write some more! Through whole group mini-lessons or individual and small group conferences, students learn strategies for selecting and organizing topics, revising, and editing. The writing process is emphasized, although the product is often published, shared, and celebrated.

Writing workshop begins with a time for "active" writing. The children work on individual pieces or work with others on a collaborative piece. Most of the time is devoted to student-selected topics; however, I do assign practice topics to encourage exploration in unfamiliar genres and styles. During this time in the workshop, you may see children writing silently and alone, children talking about a story idea, children drawing and describing characters, or children meeting with friends to get a response to a piece of their writing. I move around the room during this period, meeting with students, responding to their writing, observing, and taking notes.

After about a half-hour of active writing, I gather the children together for a "writing talk." These talks focus on strategies for becoming better writers and the "tricks of the trade." I usually am the facilitator during this time, although sometimes the children assume a leadership role and share their experiences as authors. Following "writing talk" is a period of silent writing. I write during this time, too, and the children are always curious to find out what I am writing.

The children keep their writing in files throughout the year. At the end of each year, I help them select representative samples to include in a portfolio (see figure 1.6). Conference notes and a brief analysis of their writing development are also included.

Reading Workshop
1:30–2:30

> I believe that a teacher's role is to coach, guide, or facilitate. My job is not to impart information but to show how to find that information.

We begin reading workshop with a celebration of authors. The children read aloud their own pieces of writing. I read aloud during this time each day as well. Together, the children and I have enjoyed works by such diverse authors as Patricia Polacco, Beverly Cleary, Bill Martin, and J. R. R. Tolkein.

Our extensive classroom library contains books for the emergent reader, the early reader, and the fluent reader. I help the students learn to select books that they can read on their own, help them develop

FIGURE 1.6

I have a Ant, and a cusin that live in Atlanta they Died in a house fire By a lihgted candle my cusin loved linting cadles But not Blowing them out the fire went Down the candle and lit a christmas crdament I cryed my head of I still got a one year old cusin and a 4 year old cusin But it is still not the same without Justin. Alex is my 4 year old cusin mary kathrin is my 1 year old cusin her nick name is Kati Alex and Kati are brother and sister Alex hates Kati But kiss her all the time he is werd Kati is FAT!!! I can not pick her up I still LOVE her thowe

I miss them so much my old memorys are still in my head. Justin was a lital Bossy. Juliy was my Dad's sister

After our hike!!
AFTer our hike out in The WOODS. We checked for TiCS. Ther was like Tic CiTY Ther WAS like FiFTy TiCS On e of us.

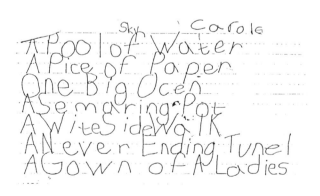

Sky Carole
A Pool of Water
A Pice of Paper
One Big Ocen
A Semaring Pot
A Wite Sidewalk
A Never Ending Tunel
A Gown of A Ladies

Writing Samples

interest in reading, and introduce them to books they may not select on their own. Taking time for this book selection process is an important part of reading workshop. The room buzzes with "book talk" during this time.

The children spend the next part of the workshop in a period of silence to practice their reading. Individual conferences held during this time help the children develop and refine good reading strategies.

Periodically throughout the year, children meet in small literature circles during reading workshop time. The circles are formed when the children select from books related by author, subject, theme, or genre. In the literature circle, the children explore topics such as an author's/illustrator's style, character development, setting, and plot. Children in the literature circles work together to share the response to their reading with the others in the class.

At the end of each reading workshop, the children make entries on a reading log that includes a brief comment on the books they read (see figure 1.7). The log becomes a part of their reading portfolio, along with my conference notes, taped readings, and self-evaluations (see figure 1.8).

Special Area
2:30–3:15

We are fortunate to have the services of teachers with special training in art, music, physical education, library skills, and foreign languages. While the children are engaged in activities with these teachers, I am busy with the never-ending record-keeping chores that are an essential part of a primary program. During this time you may find me making lesson plans, researching a Unit Study, responding to the children's writing, meeting with parents or colleagues, or organizing the anecdotal records.

It is not until 3:45, after the last child has waved good-bye for the day, that I finally have a moment for quiet reflection. As I hang Sam's latest artwork on the bulletin board, or read an urgent note from Suzanne, or pick out a book that I know Jason will enjoy, I pause for a bit to look out over the classroom. How different it is from *my* first grade room. How different it is from the rooms I organized earlier in my

FIGURE 1.7

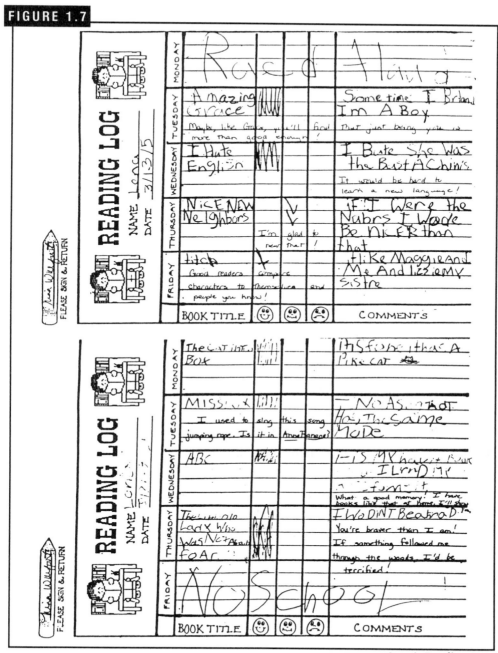

Lena's Reading Logs

FIGURE 1.8

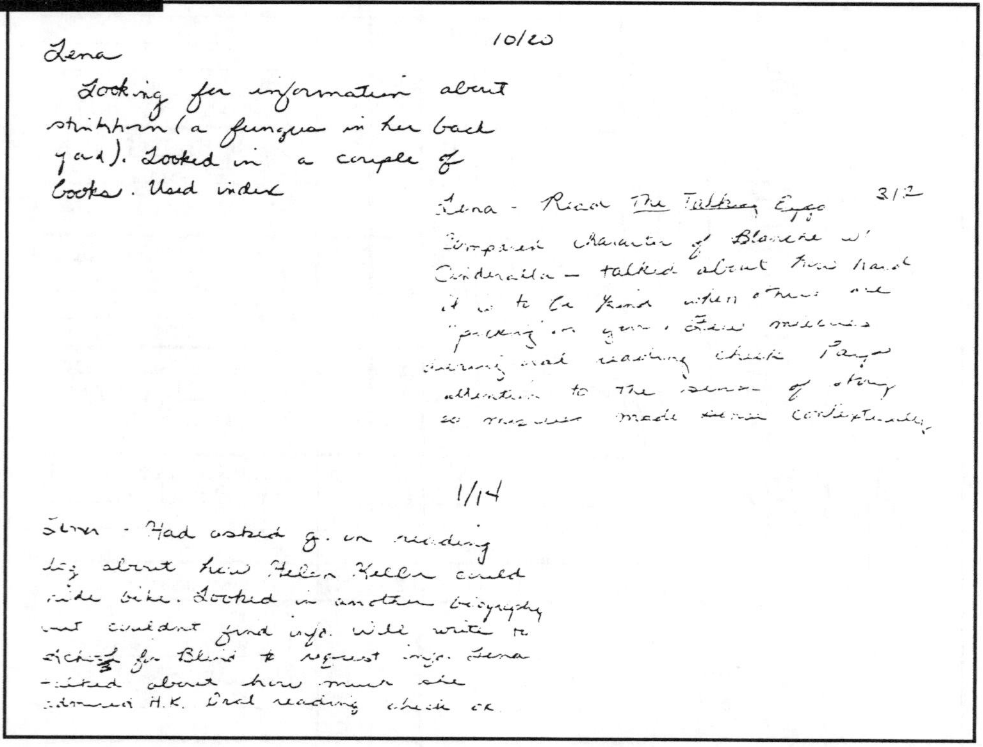

Conference notes

career. If you come into my room at the end of the day, you may find me staring off into what to you must look like distant space. But it is not. What my eyes see are the young girl and the young woman who led me to this place and who guide me still as I dare to make changes in my program. Their voices are heard. Their lessons are learned. And as our eyes meet, the young girl and the young woman nod their approval.

TEAM TEACHING: A JOURNEY OF PROFESSIONAL BONDING AND REFLECTIVE PRACTICE

BY ANNE DILL AND
GERALDINE HENDRICKS
Spencer County Elementary School
Spencer County Schools

CH3APTER

It was a hot August day, the first day of school in Kentucky. She arrived decked out in her brand new Little Mermaid outfit complete with matching backpack, watch, socks, and tennis shoes. Alexis was a beautiful six-year-old first grader. Today should be an exciting, perfect day for her. But there she sat, crying as if this day would never end. Why was she hoarding her pencils, paper, and crayons in her desk, protecting them as if there were thieves lurking in every corner of the room? No matter what we said or did to humor her, she only cried louder. When tears failed to get results, she began begging to go to the high school to be in her brother's class. We were truly sympathetic with Alexis's need for security that first day!

Just a few hours before, we had sat in that same classroom and cried as many tears as Alexis. The major difference was that we were the teachers of this class, team partners in one of the first multi-age primary units in the state. Like Alexis, we were overwhelmed with the class. During the first year of the primary program we were to discover many feelings and learning experiences that we had in common with our students. Our long journey had just begun. Both students and teachers were on the threshold of a new style of learning, different from any we had encountered.

■ THE BEGINNING . . . DO OPPOSITES ATTRACT?

When our principal first approached us about teaming in a primary unit, it didn't sound too complicated. We had taught first grade next door to each other for about eight years. We wholeheartedly agreed on the value of a whole language approach to reading, writing, and integrating subjects across the curriculum. Our classes had done joint projects over the years. We were friends. So what could possibly be the big problem with being team partners? But as we began thinking and planning for our class, we realized that we had been much too optimistic. We were both strong willed, stubborn, opinionated, and self-proclaimed authorities on all subjects. How could we work in the same room all day? Our faculty colleagues believed that we would kill each other by the end of the first week. That was assuming things went smoothly. We were opposites in so many ways. One was a strict disciplinarian, the other more laid back. One was a perfectionist in doing work and art projects for hall display. The other would display any work a child had done, even if it took an entire roll of tape pieced together. One's idea of cleaning was to throw everything into the dumpster. The other preferred to stick everything in a cabinet for future use. One researched new teaching ideas by reading every article ever printed on the subject and questioning anyone who knew anything about the technique. The other heard an idea and tried it in her class the next day. Sometimes it worked; sometimes it didn't. Could this team partnership possibly survive?

■ QUESTIONS FOLLOWED BY FEARS

Thinking about our multi-age primary room and team partnership seemed to spawn questions in every area. As the questions mounted, so did our fears. Could we allow each child to work at his or her own pace? Were we willing to step up to the responsibility of teaching young readers without the security of a manual to direct us? Did we dare risk using trade books as the basis for beginning reading and writing instruction?

It was also frightening to think about being in the room all day with another teacher watching everything. Would our partner criticize every idea or technique if it was not exactly the same process she had used in her own class? If things did not go well, would we place the entire blame on our team partner? Solutions and security in any form seemed to have vanished to another planet. Moving to a multi-age primary class and being team partners seemed to be a big, big mistake!

■ WHEN YOU LEAST EXPECT IT . . .

Collectively, our team had taught for forty years. While most of our experience was in teaching first grade, it also spanned Chapter I, high school special education, and other primary grades. With this experience, it seemed logical to assume that we would know where to begin in planning and organizing a classroom. We thought our first emphasis should be on purchasing needed equipment and designing the physical space, but we soon realized that this was a mistake. Instead, we needed to focus on our most important strength—valuing children for who they are. Doing what is best for children has been the basis for our partnership and classroom. Once we focused on this crucial realization, our minds seemed more settled, and the pieces of this primary puzzle began to fall into place. We felt organized and prepared to plunge into a learning situation that would demand that we blend our philosophies in order to provide the best environment for young minds to grow.

■ A NEW VOCABULARY WORD—WE

As we talked, worried, planned, and questioned, the value of having a partner crystallized. The concept of "we" took on new meaning. No longer did a teacher have to read, evaluate, explore, create, and plan by herself. The solitude of "I" had become the partnership of "we."

One of our first experiences with joint decision making occurred when the parents of twins requested that they be placed in our room. Usually the answer to such a request was "no," on the theory that twins should be separated so that they become less dependent on each other and develop their own interests and personalities. This time we had a different idea. The concept of family was to be a cornerstone of our primary class. We believed that if forty children, ranging in age from five to eight, were to survive and learn in one room, they would need to value and respect each other with the same consideration given in the family circle.

We wanted to have the twins and their two siblings in our class, too. To accomplish this, we began to collect research, read articles, quiz counselors and administrators, and talk with parents to get views about the best placement for all four children. When we finished one article or interview, we shared the information and thoughts. If a new idea or question crossed our minds, we wrote it down so that we could share and discuss it with our partner. We listened carefully to one another. We wanted to make the best decision for the children.

As we were working through the placement issue, a professional bond grew between us almost without our awareness. It had become a natural reflex to ask each other's opinion on all questions. The concept of "we" made making decisions simpler. Now two professionals were working with children, finding strengths and weaknesses, talking with parents and administrators, and searching for avenues for helping children learn. Knowing that two of us were searching for solutions made issues and problems of teaching seem more manageable.

Our partnership was committed to having a successful multi-age primary classroom in which children would be actively involved in learning. A bond of friendship and professional respect had grown between us. Our partnership was very solid. The fear of losing our personal and professional identities diminished. Our vision and team identity expanded as we utilized the individual strengths of each partner. The strength of our partnership gave us security and an incentive to move forward into the unknowns of multi-age primary.

■ WHO SAID CHANGE WAS EASY?

Reading the lengthy documents that accompanied KERA was the simple part. The process of change in dealing with primary school and teaming engaged brain cells that had not had a workout in years. Changing teaching patterns and methods forced us through several stages not unlike those confronted during a death or divorce. For example, we spent a lot of time in denial. Some of our colleagues suggested that we "ride out" KERA. They were sure this would be like most reforms in Kentucky education; it would die out in two or three years. Why make all the changes when we would soon be changing to something else? Next we tried to bargain. If we used only trade books to teach reading, we could still give the levels test from the basal series. That way we had the best of both worlds. Or we could use the trade books three days a week and the basals the other two. In writing, we could still do a spelling list every other week. There was no need to go hog-wild at first! After much bargaining, we became depressed.

Our depression only got worse as we realized that the list of changes we were to make for this multi-age primary classroom seemed a million miles long. Somewhere we had gotten the idea that moving to teaming and primary would involve a total of two changes. Were we ever wrong! Giving up basal readers for trade books led to giving up math workbooks for Box-It, Bag-It math manipulatives. Accepting invented spelling in journals meant moving from group phonics charts to individual strategy sessions. Deciding to have a Family Math Night to demonstrate math manipulatives to parents helped us decide to have a parent workshop for beginning readers and writers. It occurred to us that whoever said change was a process and not a product had surely taught primary or been a team partner. As each of these changes led to another change, we realized that we were capable of handling more changes when they arose. Our energies stopped fighting change, and we began focusing on creating a child-centered environment with the secure feeling of having a professional team partner working by our side.

■ 3–2–1 BLASTOFF!

After a time, we began to feel pretty superior and smug. After all, we had talked our way through the change process of accepting multi-age primary and team teaching. To be honest, it had been a difficult, trying, upsetting time for us. Yet we felt that we had grown personally as well as professionally. The time had come to sit back and pat ourselves on the back. Right? Wrong! In reality, we had only taken baby steps on what seemed to be an endless journey. When one issue was resolved, another quickly replaced it. We now truly believe there is no end or resting place to teaching primary school or being a team partner.

In many ways, this is a positive fact. We are always being forced to think through why we teach a certain way and to justify whether that technique is appropriate for young children.

We were ready to begin thinking, reading, and visiting other sites implementing multi-age primary. We read about other models, watched videos, and attended conferences about programs in Vermont, Maine, and New Zealand. Looking at many examples of physical layouts, we wanted to select the perfect layout for our classroom. We attended any whole language workshop, Bill Martin, Jr., literacy workshop, or writing workshop offered, and articles on whole language and its value in teaching beginning readers and writers became our daily reading material. The value of being a team partner kept growing each time we worked together and made decisions about our class. We learned that it is much safer to take a risk with a partner who helps you improve ideas or decide to reject them.

By the time we had decided to take some risks, trust our judgment, and think as a team, we knew some definite facts about our primary unit. We would have forty first and second graders. We chose to stay combined the entire day. We asked that a doorway be cut so that our two rooms connected. We opted to put all our desks, books, and supplies in one area called "The Office." The other room would serve as carpet area for Box-It, Bag-It math, workshops, centers, videos, and group projects.

■ IN PRIMARY WE ALL LEARN

The day we tried to fit forty desks, bookcases, files, storage cabinets, and tables into one room was the day we cried so much. We'd spent about two hours putting the desks in groups of four, then groups of six, next groups of eight. No matter how we moved them, there were just too many for one room. There was no way the children could all sit down at desks in one room. When we realized that we didn't have *our* desks in the room at all, we reached our breaking point. We looked just like our Alexis on the first day of school. When nothing seems to be going our way . . . cry. If things don't improve, cry louder!

Our multi-age primary classroom must have looked as overwhelming to Alexis that day as it did to us while we tried to fit all the desks into it. Alexis spent much of those first few days crying. During story time, authors, and drama dress-up, her crying got quieter. She enjoyed dressing up as a dancer, queen, or mama and quickly became a leader in making up plays and dialogue and directing short skits for the entire class at sharing time. Laughter and applause for her dramatic talents soon drove away Alexis's tears. She became an excellent, independent learner and helper to many of our younger students. Finding an activity she enjoyed suited Alexis much more than crying. Tears are useful but seldom the solution. Like Alexis, we looked for an alternative solution to our problem. We all learned to move on when one door closed.

Deciding what to keep and what to throw away was another big obstacle for us as team partners. Here again we were both a bit like Alexis on that first day of school. Just as she was hoarding her supplies in her desk, we were trying to hold on to all our treasures gathered through the years. Of course, we did not even touch some of them during the course of the school year, but they were tucked safely away in case we ever did find a use for them! Learning to give up total ownership is a big part of being a team partner. Our primary class got a lesson in this area, too. The children sat in clusters of four. They shared a common toolbox with four pencils, scissors, glues, erasers, crayons, and counters to ten and twenty-five. All the other "junk" stayed in their backpacks. They resisted at first, sure that there was a need for that box with 112 crayons in it. They seemed certain they would not survive the day without the pencil with a Troll head. Could any primary student cut with plain scissors when some had Big Bird heads on them? But once the students were involved in working together, they realized that it truly did not matter what tools they used. We came to the same conclusion when we started sorting through all our teaching treasures. As team partners we experienced many of the same learning, compromising, cooperating situations common in our multi-age room.

Our tables of four in many ways became mini-teams. Sharing tools gave children reasons to be responsible to the other members for keeping up with things. If someone lost a pencil, then the children's team was upset because a member did not have something to write with. We found the same to be true with memos from the office. If one of us lost a note that needed to be completed and returned, then the entire team was left out of something. Whether teacher or student, accepting responsibility for our actions when it directly affects another is a difficult and important task.

■ SURPRISE, SURPRISE, SURPRISE!!!

One area where we saw many good things happen was discipline in our class. This was an area that was a big concern for us. Because of the difference in our styles, we truly anticipated trouble. Just the opposite proved true. As a rule we encouraged the children to discuss their problems with each other rather than tattling to us. If William hit Charles, Charles had to tell William how he felt about being hurt and ask him to never do it again. In most cases, the hitting or name calling stopped after one talking session. As time went by, very little hitting or hurting of classmates occurred, and most other problems worked themselves out without teacher intervention. Just as we had learned to take the responsibility for teaching without all those manuals, our children had learned to take responsibility for their actions and behaviors. They really learned to respect the rights of others and to model the behaviors they expected of others. We saw such growth in our children in learning to work cooperatively with each other.

We saw several positive points that happened by "accident" in our class. Children automatically began giving help to classmates. We saw them help each other spell, write difficult letters, find books a classmate needed for reference, draw half a picture to finish a project for someone else. They also began recognizing each other's strengths. For writing projects, they often sought a good speller and writer. If a project needed artwork, they knew who to go to for the best pictures. If they needed more information from a resource book, they often looked up the better readers. If they were stuck on how to get going on a project, they checked with one of the better planners. We seldom pointed out the strengths of individual children; the group saw these on their own and acknowledged that everyone had some area of strength. The benefits for multi-age children multiplied throughout the entire year. We saw successes for every child in the classroom!

■ WE'VE ONLY JUST BEGUN

Teaming with another teacher did not cure all the problems associated with multi-age primary classrooms. We made so many mistakes that first year that it would take 1,000 pages to list them. We also had about that many success stories to tell. We do feel confident that our successes will grow and continue as our team partnership grows. We are also confident that we are creating a new learning environment that is well suited for young children.

Many factors enabled and encouraged our partnership and primary classroom. One important factor was being able to choose our team partner. By choosing our partner we teamed with a person that had similar philosophies about children and teaching. Secondly, selecting our own partner was an added incentive to be responsible for the success of the partnership.

Another factor in our success was the positive atmosphere our school had toward teaming and primary. This climate allowed us to take risks and supported our efforts and ideas. Had we been battling colleagues and not getting their support, we might have given up early in establishing our team and primary unit. On our "low-point" days other teachers told us something they really liked about our class and asked how to begin using the idea in their rooms. Sometimes colleagues would ask if we had thought about trying an idea they had read about or seen while visiting another primary site. These positive ideas and support gave us the encouragement we needed to move on.

We have always been committed to the idea of nongraded primary and recognized its appropriateness for children. Yet in all honesty, we could not write this without mentioning the personal sacrifice it takes or the stress level teachers experience while working in primary. We have asked much of our families while we worked to establish our team and primary class. There is no doubt in our minds or hearts that our families are silent partners in our team and primary unit. Most days we continue to question if the sacrifices are worthwhile. But our commitment remains strong and is reinforced by the rewards.

Both students and teachers reap many rewards from the Kentucky primary school model. Our students work well together, keep seeking more information if their interest is piqued, and maintain a *can do* attitude that will keep them learning throughout their lives.

The rewards are valuable for our learning, too. We very often say that there is never a day that we do not learn something new. We have come to see ourselves as professionals, accepting responsibility for our teaching. We are willing to take risks to change if our children are to be the benefactors. Recognizing the value of constant refining and questioning of our teaching methods has been most beneficial to us. Just as learning is not a race but a journey for children, being a team partner in multi-age primary is a journey. We feel we are on a road that has many bumps, curves, detours, and hills yet to come. We see the road signs with more changes and avenues to explore. These avenues hold promise for helping children continue their journey into learning.

As we were trying to meet the deadline for this chapter, we worked daily on our writing while the children wrote in their journals. We explained to them that it was difficult to get the words just right and that we were having to edit and rewrite. Instantly little hands began to shoot up all around the room. They were volunteering to do the drawings for our chapter. They knew well that neither of us was an artist, but they could draw and wanted to help us! Our two-member team had grown into a forty-two-member team during the year. The spirit of teamwork was overflowing in our children.

Working and learning together has been a scary yet exciting learning experience for us all. Our Alexis became a confident, excellent student and leader in our class. We, as team partners, have grown as well and continue to be excited about new ideas and directions for our multi-age primary class. And like Alexis, we are on a learning journey with many unknown avenues to explore. Together, we look ahead to the new roads and opportunities before us.

SEA OF CHANGES: FINDING SUNKEN TREASURES IN SHARK-INFESTED WATERS

BY CATHY COOL
Campbell County Schools

C H A P T E R 4

My dad had always wanted to be a professional comedian. Growing up, I can remember many times when he would be upstairs pacing back and forth practicing his routines over and over. By the time he was ready to perform his routine for an audience, I truly believe that any one of my brothers or sisters, my mom, and probably Tippy, our dog, could have done the routine. Well, maybe I'm exaggerating. Tippy always messed up the punch lines.

Now that I am an adult, something will trigger one of those old comedy routines, and one of his jokes will come back to haunt me. As I think of change, in the back of my mind I can hear my dad talking about a rather ominous scene. Imagine if you will . . . it is midnight. We find ourselves peering into the window of a laboratory in an old castle. As we listen in, we can hear the mad scientist yelling, "I'm changing! Igor, *I'M CHANGING!* Igor, how many times have I told you to shut the blinds when I'm changing!"

I thought of this punch line, and it occurred to me that change means different things to different people. Some people fear it, while others continually change. As I looked at the varying levels of acceptance to the way KERA has changed education in Kentucky, the teachers who always used phrases like, "I never did the same thing from one year to the next" or, "I would get bored doing the same things year after year" are the teachers who have more readily accepted changes KERA has brought. I am a teacher who invites change. After having survived my first year of teaching, I saw the same stories in our fifth grade reader coming up again and found myself trying to do "something different from the way we did it last year." One day I went to the principal of the Catholic elementary school where I was teaching and said, "Sister, there is a story in our reader about cave paintings, and I was wondering if I could build a cave in the hallway."

And she said, "A cave?!" There was a slight hesitation and a hint of both excitement and terror in her voice. She paused for a moment and then calmly asked, "Will it be safe?" "Oh, yes, Sister." "Will you clean it up after you are finished?" "Oh, yes, Sister!" She had no idea what monster she had unleashed. Or maybe she knew more about the future of education than she led me to believe.

That was about five years ago. This year at Cold Spring Elementary a team of teachers constructed an ocean in the whole Primary hallway. KERA has changed things. Back in the "cave days," I can remember other teachers saying, "What is that 'Crazy Miss Cool' doing down there?" Now that KERA has washed ashore, an ocean in the hallway is an expected thing, rather than an unusual one. Now other teachers are saying, "What is that crazy group of primary teachers doing down there?" This illustrates

Rule #1: All people in a school change at their own speed, in their own way, and when they are ready.

Do you remember the rule we were taught about crossing the street: "Stop, Look, and Listen"? To me, teaching is a lot like crossing the street. I often catch myself questioning my teaching. "Stop and wait a minute. Why didn't the kids get this?" Then I look. "What am I doing?" (I do not say, "What am I doing wrong?") Then I listen. I listen to the children by saying, "Explain to me what you think I have taught you." I listen to other teachers and ask, "How do *you* do it?" I often read the research about what I am attempting. Then I decide how I want to make a change in my teaching. I look at change as constant growth. KERA has *not* said to me that the way I teach is wrong. It has showed me ways I can grow.

If you decide that it is safe to cross the street with me, I will let you "look in my windows" while I am changing. You will see how my teaching has evolved.

■ ADOPTING THE CONTINUOUS PROGRESS CONCEPT

I taught Casey in 1991 when he was in second grade and again the following year in my primary classroom that contained seven- and eight-year-olds. Casey is a dashing young man with an incredible talent for art. And he might tell you within the first five minutes you meet that he knows anything and everything about sharks.

Last year when Casey first came to our class, he had two positions: drawing sharks and folding his arms. Casey informed me that he did not have to do schoolwork because he was going to be an artist, and an artist did not need to know how to read and write. He especially resisted workbook pages.

One day in particular stands out in my mind as a real turning point for me. Casey was being his usual self and refusing to do a workbook page. I was being my usual self and telling Casey in my "teacher voice" that completing the work would help him become a better reader and that he needed to be a good reader to do well in life. When I reached my limit, I threw in the old, "If you don't finish the paper, you may not go outside for recess." He looked at me. I walked away. Out of the corner of my eye, I saw him quickly write words on the paper and then push it away. I walked over to him preparing to tell him that he would have to do it over. I was sure he had just written in any answer to complete the paper, because even the top readers in the class took at least ten minutes to complete it.

His answers were correct. They were *all* correct. I thanked him. He went outside. He got what he wanted, and I got what I wanted. But I kept thinking of that incident for weeks. It bugged me.

My mind flooded with thoughts. What was accomplished? What did Casey learn? Then I began thinking about the other children in my class and the way I used the workbooks. I would introduce the lesson. The class would practice the skill and then they would do the workbook page. Then I would grade it. The funny thing was I knew which children would answer correctly. Some would do very well. Others would do well as long as they could ask me a question or two. Some would end up having to redo the page because of a low score. I stopped. I looked. I listened.

Rule 2: Teachers need to provide experiences in which all children can achieve success.

The primary program has permitted me to admit that the children in my classroom are of different abilities and are on different levels. Since I had children of different ages in my room, assigning the same workbook page to the entire class was not appropriate. What seems more reasonable now are activities that address each student's present need.

The way I approach reading has changed. During what I call Workshop Time, small groups of students engage in activities together, but the expectations for each student may be different. For example, four students play a card game similar to Rummy. The object of the game is to collect four cards that belong together—one main idea and three details. Among the four students are two or three children who are capable readers who need to learn about main ideas and details and one or two children who are emergent readers. The capable readers are allowed to help the emergent readers read the information on each card. At the end of the activity, the readers identify main ideas and details, and the emergent readers read all of the cards in their matching set.

Now life with Casey has changed from being a battle of wills each day. Using the trade books appropriate to his reading level, Casey is reading about sharks as well as other topics and is writing reports about what interests him. Using the writing process, Casey is improving his writing skills, but he is also using his wonderful artistic ability to illustrate his stories. I still have to use my teacher voice, but the treasure I am defending is not a completed workbook page. It is Casey. And my goal for him is to continue to grow and improve himself.

■ UNDERSTANDING DEVELOPMENTALLY APPROPRIATE PRACTICE: FROM TEXTBOOKS TO TRADE BOOKS

I was excited to be able to use trade books instead of basal readers in the classroom. Children are much more interested in reading books they choose rather than a story they are required to read because it is next in the reader. During Workshop Time groups work with stories and activities that pertain to the present theme. Books related to the theme are very popular.

Reading workshop is a time when kids read trade books, write reports, do story maps, prepare projects to share a book with the class, or read with me. It is generally a quiet time, but a busy one. When I first started reading workshop it was new to me because I generally used trade books only for reading aloud and silent reading time. But when I began to use trade books as the basis of the reading curriculum, I could feel the children's interest growing. It was exciting.

As I walk through the room, I listen to the children. There is energy. They are happy. They are interested in reading. One day, Megan was looking for a book to read and Ben said, "I know a good one." I thought to myself, "Ben is so excited about reading that he is sparking another student's interest in a book. This trade book stuff is not that hard." Then Ben brought the book to Megan and said, "Here. Just do this one. It's e-e-e-easy." That blast that you just heard was my bubble bursting. Megan can read novels.

Rule #3: You need to set limits.

Since then each of the books in my classroom library has been color coded according to reading levels. Students may read books on or above their assigned level during reading workshop time. They may read any book for pleasure. I have so much to learn. Students are not the only ones who will be expected to constantly improve because of the changes from KERA.

■ LEARNING THE MULTI-AGE CONCEPT

I tune pianos as a part-time job. I visit many homes and meet many people. Sometimes in between the twangs and twists of the piano strings, it comes up in conversation that I teach school full time. Inevitably, the first question people ask me is, "What grade do you teach?" Sometimes I just say "primary" or "second and third grade." But if I am not too tired from making math activities, evaluating writing samples, reading journal entries, writing narrative report cards, or keeping late hours, I take a deep breath and begin, "Well, Kentucky has this reform."

Their responses vary, but many times I hear something like, "Why do they want to mix the kids like that?" This is such a hard question to answer in the hour or so that it takes to tune a piano. It is almost something you have to experience to understand.

I have witnessed so many "little teachers" in my room that I find it hard to choose one story to illustrate the way students benefit from being in a multi-aged classroom. Many times I have looked over at a table and seen Shannon (an older capable writer) reading a story that she is in the process of writing to Traci (a younger emergent writer). Traci thinks that Shannon is the cat's meow. So Traci benefits because she is listening to Shannon's more mature example, and Shannon benefits because she has an interested audience with whom to test her writing. It is not just the "olders" helping the "youngers." I remember Paul, a seven-year-old, helped Brad, an eight-year-old, with the number of zeroes in a million. Tyler, a younger child, was the only one who could supply the term "classify" during a lesson about animals. Waylon, a younger child, helped the other older students in his group with the names of some of the states on a U.S. map.

Rule #4: Recognize that children in multi-aged classes have varied abilities.

I began writing this section hoping to answer the question, "What can six- and seven-year-olds learn from eight- and nine-year-olds?" That is a key question in Kentucky education now. Then I began searching my experiences for the perfect anecdote to illustrate the answer. I thought of Shannon and Megan and Tyler and Paul and Waylon and all of the other "little teachers" in my room. I stopped, looked, and listened. The little teachers taught this "big teacher" something.

A multi-aged classroom demands that the teacher focus on the multi-abilities in the classroom. Therefore, the goals and objectives of the activities, the assessment, the curriculum, and the entire environment must address the needs and abilities of each individual student. So the question is no longer, "What can six- and seven-year-olds learn from eight- and nine-year-olds?" but, "What can children learn from children?" This shifts the focus back on learning rather than teaching or the textbook. The goal is the *child* rather than the curriculum. And the outcome is *learning* rather than passing to the next grade.

■ DEVELOPING A VIEW OF CHANGE

I started the chapter by telling you about my dad. Thanks to Dad and his sense of humor, I think I have learned in life to make rainbows from rain and lemonade from lemons and to look at the good things about KERA. So I think it is only fair that I give my mom equal time.

For much of her life, Mom has been the "straight one." At first, you may think that being the straight one is not a very important job, but the straight one is just as important as the one with the jokes: Laurel and Hardy, Abbott and Costello, Peanut Butter and Jelly. It is a balance. You cannot have one without the other. So as I look at the good things KERA has brought, I also know the difficulties that have followed, primarily the need to *change.*

Mom has had to deal with a lot of changes in her life. And watching how she deals with change, I have learned some things that have helped me continue when I feel like running back to the past.

Rule #5: To change you have to have the courage to keep your blinds open.

First, you have to be brave enough to let go. It is scary to tread through unknown territory. I had to believe that I was going to a better place, and I do believe it. Second, you have to trust yourself. Even though KERA has changed things, I am still me. I feel that I was a good teacher before KERA, so I will still be one after KERA. Third, you should not be afraid to say you need help. I was nervous about letting other people know that something I was doing was not working. I wandered across the hall to talk to fellow primary teachers after one of those "days to end all days." I walked in and saw such nice things in their rooms and just knew their programs all worked out. But as we talked, I learned that they sometimes have one of "those days" too, and that has helped us build trust and support for one another. I forgave myself for not knowing everything, and now we help each other grow by exchanging ideas. Lastly, you have to begin. KERA equals change to me, and the way I see it, I am just beginning.

Name: Brittany Palo
Date: 10/11-10/15

PLEASE SIGN & RETURN

MATH LOG

MONDAY	TUESDAY	WEDNESDAY	THURSDAY	COMMENTS
Game Selected: Spin a half dollar	Game Selected:	Game Selected: Part Fund Shop	Game Selected:	Comments and Observations: In Chapter Three, Brittany will be working on mental math strategies; addition and subtraction with regrouping and problem solving;
Assignment: 7/5	Assignment: Chapter 3 Pretest	Assignment: Help Gate with Math	Assignment: 83 problems	
Choosing an operation	Two Digit Addition & Subtraction	Helped Gato with the concept of trading 10's for 1's	Addition: Mental Math	
89%	6/21	70% to 88%	67%	

SECTION 2

AUTHENTIC ASSESSMENT AND CONTINUOUS PROGRESS

> We are observing the children and listening to them. We are learning so much about how they think, operate, and perceive themselves. This firsthand experience gives us the foundation and confidence we need to design tools and curricula that fit our students and their individual needs.
>
> Kris Gregory, Gayle Moore,
> Vickie Wheatley, Anna Yancey
> LaGrange Elementary

This section addresses the variety of ways teachers document students' academic and social progress and how they report information to parents. The classrooms represented in this section include children of varied backgrounds and experiences, economic levels, ethnicities, abilities and disabilities, and learning styles. The teachers describe how they assess and meet the needs of the variety of children in their classrooms by linking assessment to decisions about the most appropriate instruction.

ASSESSMENT IN A NONGRADED PRIMARY PROGRAM: DISCOVERING CHILDREN'S VOICES AND TALENTS

BY KRIS GREGORY, GAYLE MOORE, VICKIE WHEATLEY, AND ANNA YANCEY
LaGrange Elementary
Oldham County Schools

CHAPTER 5

■ ACCEPTING THE CHALLENGE

Can I be the teacher today? (Allen, age 5)

Look! I wrote it and it makes sense this time. (Jane, age 6)

I think Richard deserves a happy note today because his coat and backpack are not on the floor. (Kelly, age 7)

Our greatest joys and our greatest fears this year stem from the simple, yet pivotal, fact that we are shifting our whole focus in assessment. Last year we read about becoming "kidwatchers" (Goodman, 1985). This year we are experiencing it firsthand. We are also guiding the students to become kidwatchers themselves and helping them assess their own progress (and each other's), as illustrated in the quotations above. The joy of this new experience is reflected in our busy, active classrooms and in the voices of the children. We are seeing children gain self-confidence through participation and empowerment in the classroom. Our fears creep in after the children are gone. In the quiet of our empty classrooms, we ask ourselves:

- How will we assess reading and math progress without the use of basal readers or math texts?

- What if a child moves to another school? Will he or she "measure up"? Does it matter?

- If, through assessment, we see that a child is not reading at the end of early primary, what should we do?

- Is it OK to have a free-choice time and allow the older children to just play? How do we assess what they are learning during this time?

The underlying question seems to be, "Are we capable of making our own decisions about what we teach and how we assess?" We are realizing that the answer is, "Yes, we are capable, and yes, we must make these decisions." Each day we become more comfortable in our roles as decision makers and assessors.

KERA has emphasized and mandated that primary teachers use new methods of assessment in their nongraded programs. The major change is a shift in focus from quantitative, end-of-quarter/semester/chapter assessment to qualitative, continuous assessment of each child's progress. For example, rather than using and scoring standardized work-book pages and end-of-the-book tests to assess a child's reading abilities, we keep ongoing anecdotal records of what we see children doing when they are actively reading. We note reading strategies and skills they are using to make sense of print on a daily or weekly basis.

Because of KERA's emphasis on qualitative, continuous assessment, we are observing the children and listening to them. We are learning so much about how they think, operate, and perceive themselves. This firsthand experience gives us the foundation and confidence we need to design assessment tools and curricula that fit our students and their individual needs. We are also supported in our new roles by continued professional development, a supportive, innovative principal, and parents who have faith in us.

∎ SETTING THE STAGE

Our primary program has unique components and is, we think, an excellent model. In our program we have twelve first-year five-year-olds and twelve six-year-olds. The first-year children attend school only half the day, and during that time each teacher has an aide. For the other half of the day, the teachers have only six-year-olds. Each classroom teacher is paired with a teacher of seven- and eight-year-olds, and that entire primary group is a family. The paired teachers periodically plan activities that involve all the students. Also, at the end of the school year, the six-year-olds move as a group to their seven- and eight-year-old family group.

Our school is located in LaGrange, Kentucky, a small town in Oldham County that serves as a bedroom community for Louisville. Students at our school are a diverse group. They come from a wide variety of home environments and socioeconomic levels. However, 45 percent of our students are designated "at-risk" because of their low socioeconomic level. Just as our students are multi-age and multi-ability, so is our team of teachers. There is a twenty-nine-year age span from the youngest to the oldest, and among the four of us, we have seventy-four years of teaching experience, which ranges from preschool to twelfth grade. Though our wide range of experiences has helped us on our journey toward nongraded primary, we often feel like first year teachers. We are changing, growing, and learning to "throw out the garbage" and adapt the good things along the way. Despite our diverse backgrounds and personalities, we all agree that multi-age, multi-ability is the way to go, for kids as well as adults!

We are all involved in many projects and studies. Although we have discovered that these experiences are important, a positive attitude is crucial in successfully making the transition to nongraded primary. Some of the programs in which we are involved include the Ohio Valley Educational Consortium Project Discovery, aimed at helping teachers assess students and find/develop their gifts and talents, and KELP (Kentucky Early Learning Profile), whose purpose is to help teachers do qualitative continuous assessment of the whole child. Our professional growth continues through a research grant studying teachers' transitions to nongraded primary, involvement in college courses, and researching and writing children's books.

■ MORNING ACTIVITIES/ASSESSMENT STRATEGIES

In this section we will paint a picture of a typical day. After each example of student work, we will discuss how we might use the example to assess student progress.

The children breeze into the classroom, eager to share something about their personal experiences since the day before. Rob tells a story about his little brothers, while the other children are making lunch choices, putting their coats and backpacks away, and getting ready for the day. The first period of the day begins as children select the materials they need to get to work. For example, Brian chooses to work in his writing journal:

FIGURE 5.1

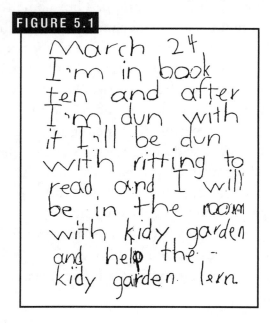

March 24
I'm in book
ten and after
I'm dun with
it I'll be dun
with ritting to
read and I will
be in the room
with kidy garden
and help the
kidy garden lern

Later, to gain information and insight into his thinking process, we might ask Brian in an informal conference how he plans to help the younger students and how he feels about the Write to Read Program. We would also mention that he is using apostrophes and capital letters correctly. In our anecdotal records, we would note his sense of accomplishment and his interest in helping his peers as well as the readability of his entry.

Through journal entries like this and the additional samples, we see and assess feelings, interests, attitudes, and personal and academic growth. Along with each work sample, we added some comments about strategies and skills we've noted.

FIGURE 5.2

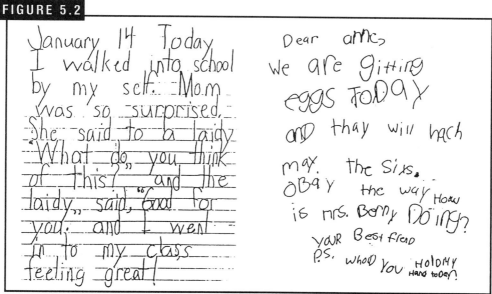

- **Good self-assessment/snapshot of her feelings**
- **Almost conventional spelling**
- **Correct use of punctuation and quotation marks**

- **Good example of personal letter**
- **Correct use of question marks and postscript**
- **Good "voice"**

FIGURE 5.3

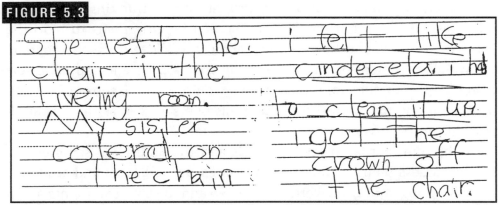

She left the chair in the living room. My sister colered on the chair.

I felt like Cinderela. i had to clean it up. I got the crown off the chair.

"I feel like Cinderella." Neat way to describe how *you* felt.

FIGURE 5.4

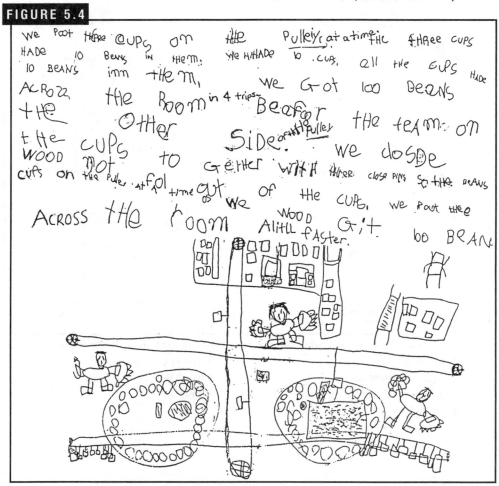

We poot three cups on the pulley, r at a time the three cups hade 10 beans in them. we hade 10 cups. all the cups hade 10 beans imm them, acrozz the room in 4 trips we got 100 beans beafor the team on the other side of the pulley the cups wood not to gether with three close pins so the beans cups on the puley at 1 time out we of the cups, we poot three across the room wood alittl faster. git. 100 bean

Descriptive, sequential explanation and picture of "pulley" performance task.
Transitional spelling with some good self-correction/editing.

The following samples mark a journey from beginning "scribble writing" to the use of formula sentences such as "I see the cat," to writing personal experience stories using invented spelling, and finally to writing stories that incorporate conventions of print and standard spelling. We use developmental literacy scales developed from the work of Clay (1975), Sulzby (1985; 1992), and others to guide us in determining what each child knows and to help us while preparing him or her to move developmentally. (See figure 5.6 for the developmental scales.)

Over in the reading area Donna and Kathy sit down to read *The Very Hungry Caterpillar:* Donna begins,

"On Tuesday he ate through two apples," said Donna.

"No, said Kathy, "that's not right. Look here" (pointing to the words that say "two pears").

Donna still looks skeptical, so Kathy points to the pictures instead.

"Oh, yeah," said Donna, "On Tuesday he ate through two pears." They continue reading together, and we do not intrude on this exchange. We note in our records that Donna is using memory and pictures to "read," while Kathy is focusing on the print.

Meanwhile, back at the art center, Sallie, Carrie, Megan, and Ronald are making paper bag puppets to use in a dramatization of a story they have read. Through activities and projects of this type, we are able to assess children's interactions, leadership abilities, imagination, creativity, and comprehension of the story. We get a feel for the modalities (art, drama, language, mathematical reasoning) individual children use. This provides us with information vital to structuring the learning environment.

While observing at the arts center, we note that Megan is confident and uses language naturally, while Sallie struggles to remember exactly how her part is worded. Carrie's interpretation of the bumblebee through her embellishment of the paper bag puppet is an indication of her sense of creativity and her attention to detail.

After this morning block of time, our students go to the art, music, or P.E. teacher for a fifty-minute activity block. We use this time to schedule parent conferences and to plan either as a team or individually.

The next period is an hour and twenty minutes of flexible time when we focus on topics or themes of interest to individual children. As

FIGURE 5.5

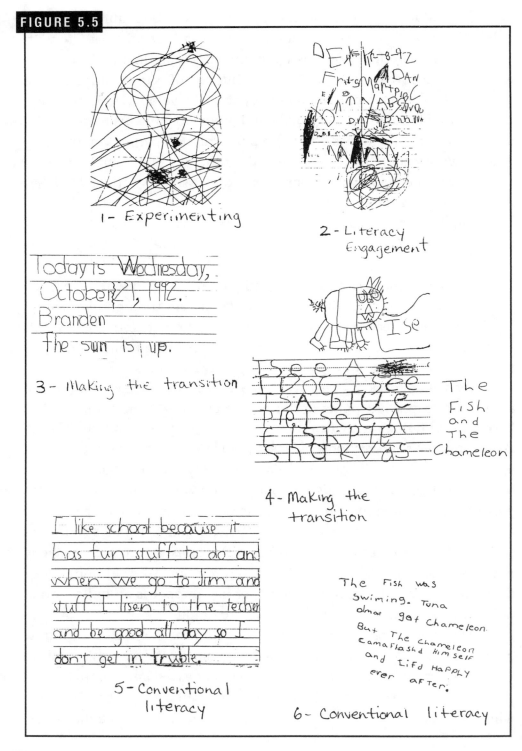

1- Experimenting

2- Literacy
Engagement

Today is Wednesday,
October 21, 1992.
Branden
The sun is up.

3- Making the transition

I se

See A
Frog I see
A blue
Pig I see A
Fish pig
SADK VAS

The
Fish
and
The
Chameleon

4- Making the
transition

I like school because it
has fun stuff to do and
when we go to Jim and
stuff I lisen to the techer
and be good all day so I
don't get in truble.

5- Conventional
literacy

The Fish was
swiming. Tuna
olmat got Chameleon.
But The Chameleon
Camaflashd Him self
and Lifd HAPPLY
ever afTer.

6- Conventional literacy

FIGURE 5.6

EMERGENT LITERACY DEVELOPMENT:
READING AND WRITING ACTIONS

(Compiled from the work of Clay, Gentry, Purcell-Gates, and Sulzby)

Experimenting

Book handling, interest in stories

Drawing, construction, scribbling

Literacy Engagement: Making Meaning

Reading pictures
—oral-like language
—written-like language
—memory

Controlled scribbling
—wavy-like
—letter-like

Letter-like units

Letters—random

Letters—patterned

Making the Transition

Reading the print
—from memory
—aspectually (e.g., focusing only on sounds or known words)

Writing the known (e.g., Writing formula sentences)

Spelling inventively
—semi-phonemic level (BSKT—basket)
—phonemic level (GYNS AT WRK—genius at work)
—transitional (knighte—kite)

Conventional Literacy

Child can read a text never seen before and make sense of it.

Child can write something others can read.

IMPORTANT: These are not discrete stages; all overlap, and some children may exhibit several behaviors from a variety of categories in one day. Experience and their own purpose determines what they do. However, this can be viewed as a general, or global, development progression. Expect to find exceptions!

groups work on individual projects, one way we assess learning progress is to pull up a chair beside a group and take anecdotal records. We do this in several different ways. One teacher keeps records on 5" × 7" cards that have been overlapped and taped on a clipboard (see figure 5.7). Another takes notes on computer address labels and then sticks them onto the 5" × 7" card. Still another uses a Xerox sheet marked off into grids that are labeled with each child's name and then transfers notes to the cards.

We evaluate children during the individual project time, but children also evaluate each other as they present their projects to the group. The questions generated by their peers give the presenters feedback, reinforcement, and a new sense of purpose as they see themselves as a part of a community of learners.

Jackie and Betty, after tracing an outline of their bodies on butcher paper, drew internal organs on their life-sized bodies. They learned from the process. But it was the interest, enthusiasm, and questioning of other group members during their presentation that spurred them to really learn about their subject through research. Their classmates generated questions such as:

- What is that thing underneath the heart?
- What makes your arm bend?
- Why are there blood vessels in the lungs?

FIGURE 5.7

Developed By Teachers at LaGrange Elementary

READING:

* Using pictures & story language to "read" The Three Little Pigs (indl.)
* Using mostly pictures but beginning to focus on words (pointing to words in story Very Hungry Caterpillar (w/ a partner)
* Finding simple words that are repeated on a page (little, red, she) Little Red Hen (w/ teacher)

MATH:

- Copied and extended a simple ABAB pattern w/ unifix cubes (w/ small group)
- Correctly counted 10 unifix cubes using 1-1 correspondence (pointed to each block as she counted) individually
- Adds "1 more" w/ unifix cubes up to 10 (w/ teacher help)

PERSONAL & SOCIAL GROWTH:

* Parallel Play - at block center played next to Sim but not with him (Center Time)
* At recess played with John on the playground equipment - pretended they were sharks
* Retold story in front of small group (on her own)

LANGUAGE:

- Expresses ideas fof interest to a friend (so he can understand)
- Can retell and innovate on a simple story (The Three Bears) w/ prompts

TEACHER'S NAME: __________ SCHOOL YEAR: __________

STUDENT'S NAME: __________ R 9-15 10-21 11-15 M 8-24 9-21 10-15 P 9-6 10-24 11-15 La 9-30 10-15

These sent Jackie and Betty scrambling back to their resources to find the answers for an interested, appreciative audience.

In another class children made reports on wild animals in preparation for a field trip to the woods. They wrote them in the first person to stimulate interest. In the report shown in figure 5.8, Freddy the Fox prepared a second page when his peers asked:

- What color are your eyes?
- What are baby foxes called?

FIGURE 5.8

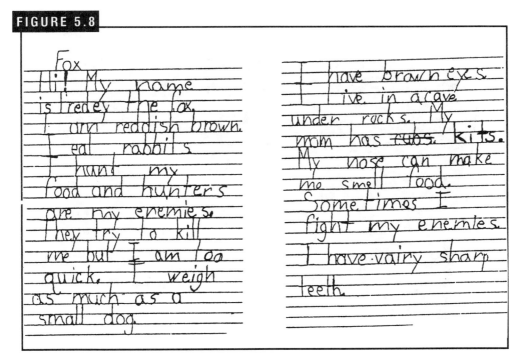

It was the other students—their community of learners—that led to this further interest, research, and learning on the part of Freddy. We find it exciting, rewarding, and comforting that children are helping and supporting each other as learners and assessors in our classrooms.

■ AFTERNOON ACTIVITIES/ASSESSMENT STRATEGIES

Our five-year-olds arrive with their backpacks, coat bags, lunch boxes, pictures, presents, and dandelions for the teacher. Fortunately, an aide comes with them! Again, each classroom operates a little differently, but we all spend time reading, singing, and sharing. The exciting thing about this time of day is that all of the children are engaged in book talk; no matter where they are as readers they are able to share books, make connections between literature and their lives, and simply enjoy the pleasures of reading. We notice that many of these young children are reading beyond traditional expectations of them. It's like the story about the bumblebee, who, according to the laws of physics, should be unable to fly. But no one ever told *him* that he couldn't, so he does, beautifully.

The time allotment for lunch and recess is forty-five minutes. This is an ideal time to discuss and model good problem-solving and social strategies. Our children have a wide range of abilities in their interpersonal relationships. We often ask children who demonstrate good social strategies to model or role-play with other children who need to develop better interpersonal strategies.

For example, we noticed one day at recess that John used the strategy of "looking on" before approaching Mark and Angela, who were arguing over the ball. He watched them for a few seconds and then walked over and said, "How about if we share the ball? Go get Debbie, Erik, and Ian and let's play dodge ball." That afternoon during our citizenship meeting, we asked John to role-play his strategy for the class. In this way we use the strengths we observe in the children to further instruct other children.

After recess, we have an hour block of time. During this time, we do theme-related activities, have free-choice time and centers (blocks, games, art, reading and listening, writing, math, board games, drama, and so on), and language-related activities. Because we have an aide in the afternoon, we are able to form small groups for special needs, interests, and skills. As they are actively engaged in their learning, we circulate around the room observing children and taking anecdotal records. We record observations like:

- Brian watches John build a block castle, suggests adding a tower to the front, then sits down and helps build.
- Brandon copies patterns from a pattern block Workjob card, then tries a new pattern of his own.
- Linda and Sue are attempting to make a rhythm pattern on the glockenspiel.

All the notes we make relate to children's skill development, learning strategies, or interests. We realize that next year we need to identify the context in which the observation occurred (i.e., small group, large group, pairs, or independently; teacher or child directed; teacher or child initiated, and so on). This should help us make more sense of our notes!

As we circulate through the room during center time, we also use checklists for basic concepts and skills such as knowing names, addresses, phone numbers, and birth dates and for noting reading strategies (i.e., sounding out words, using context/meaning, reading from memory, self-correcting, and so on) and math concepts (counting, number sense, shapes, adding/subtracting, sorting/classifying, number recognition, and so on) and other basic information. During the remaining thirty minutes, half of our children go to the IBM Write to Read Center, and the other half work on math strategies in the classroom.

The last fifteen minutes of the day are spent passing out papers, organizing the room, distributing materials to go home, and having the children line up for buses. Even this time is full of learning: organizational skills, number recognition, sequencing, and responsibility are all actively modeled and learned.

■ REPORTING TO PARENTS

Because we are looking at the whole child and reporting to parents about social and emotional growth and a broadened educational agenda, the process of assessment and evaluation is much more time intensive and complex than it used to be. The resources we use when preparing to fill out a progress report consist of a child's:

- writing portfolio
- book log
- writing journal
- work samples from content areas/performance tasks
- previous progress reports
- anecdotal records

The writing portfolio contains samples of each child's best writing, including stories, letters, personal narratives, and research and writing about other content areas, including math. The book log is a dated record of books and poems a child has read. The writing journal contains daily entries on any topic of interest to the child. Our anecdotal records include information about social growth, reading and math strategies and skills, problem solving strategies, and personal interests.

Our progress report was developed by a team of primary teachers at our school during the summer of 1992. We chose this reporting device to more accurately reflect the KERA goals and academic expectations (see figure 5.9).

The progress report is distributed five times during the year, and the first progress report was explained to parents at a mandatory parent conference. Teachers and parents could also choose to replace one progress report with a conference. In addition to progress reports, we

FIGURE 5.9

OLDHAM COUNTY BOARD OF EDUCATION / LAGRANGE ELEMENTARY SCHOOL
PRIMARY SCHOOL PROGRESS REPORT

Student:

Yearly Attendance____ ____ ____ ____

Yearly Tardies____ ____ ____ ____

Teacher:

Date____ ____ ____ ____

| • consistently demonstrates skill
✓ occasionally demonstrates skill
- does not demonstrate skill | P Progressing with help
B Beginning the skill
D Developing the skill
H Help needed at home | I Independent use of skill
N Not Yet
C Concerned - conference needed
Blank - does not apply at this time |

PERSONAL AND SOCIAL GROWTH

____ Exhibits self confidence
____ Respects rights of others
____ Follows directions well
____ Listens and responds
____ Complies with classroom rules
____ Works and plays cooperatively
____ Works and plays independently
____ Takes care of materials, work, and personal belongings
____ Values own work
____ Seeks help when needed
____ Works neatly
____ Is curious about learning
____ Is willing to accept challenges

MUSIC

____ Shows interest in music
____ Demonstrates skill development

ART

____ Shows interest in art
____ Demonstrates skill development

PHYSICAL EDUCATION

____ Shows interest in PE
____ Demonstrates skill development

COMMENTS:

LISTENING AND SPEAKING

____ Speaks distinctly
____ Expresses ideas clearly
____ Pays attention to others
____ Participates in discussions
____ Presents prepared information orally
____ Listens purposefully

LANGUAGE ARTS: WRITING

____ Expresses ideas
____ Writes own sentences/paragraphs
____ Writes for different purposes
____ Proofreads and corrects work
____ Shares writing with group
____ Uses reference materials
____ Forms letters and numerals correctly
____ Spaces letters and words correctly
____ Uses invented/book spelling

REFERENCE SKILLS

____ Recognizes the different parts of a book
____ Chooses appropriate reference material (dictionary, newspaper, encyclopedia, atlas, magazine)
____ Can find answer to question in reference material
____ Can summarize information into his/her own words

COMMENTS:

LANGUAGE ARTS: READING

____ Interested in books
____ Identifies capitals/lower case letters
____ Retells a story
____ Understands what is read to him/her
____ Selects and reads appropriate material for his/her ability level
____ Reads fluently
____ Recognizes and reads sight words
____ Uses reading strategies

____ Reads with expression
____ Reads directions
____ Raises insightful questions

COMMENTS:

MATHEMATICS

____ Shows interest in math
____ Counts to ____
____ Counts sets
____ Recognizes 4 basic shapes
____ Demonstrates number sense
____ Observes, collects and organizes data
____ Recognizes and creates patterns
____ Whole number computation

____ Uses appropriate math skill to solve problem

____ Can apply math to real life experiences
____ Can communicate mathematical ideas in oral and written form

COMMENTS:

develop learning goals for each child and share them with parents in November (see figure 5.10).

Some examples of learning goals for five- and six-year-olds are:

• use manipulatives to develop concepts of less, more, addition, subtraction

• retell stories using picture clues, specific phrases, and/or language used in the stories

• write original texts (five or more sentences long) describing or explaining a subject

As children reach these goals throughout the year, new goals are added to replace them, and parents are notified of the update.

One of our most important teacher goals is to keep open communication with parents. Parents are encouraged to: volunteer in the classroom, chaperone field trips, eat lunch with their child, help out at recess, and attend various types of classroom programs and performances. Extra

FIGURE 5.10

LAGRANGE ELEMENTARY SCHOOL
STUDENT INSTRUCTIONAL PLAN

CHILD'S NAME _____

TEACHER _____

DATE _____

LEARNING GOALS:

1.

2.

3.

4.

5.

Teacher's Signature _____

Parent's Signature(s) _____

Child's Signature _____

Developed by LaGrange Elementary Teachers

parent conferences are scheduled as needed by the parent or teacher. Another teacher goal is to send home weekly newsletters so parents know what's going on at school.

All of this school/family participation helps parents better understand nongraded primary, goal setting, progress reports, assessment techniques, and how these are incorporated into a typical school day. It helps all of us better understand and assist the whole child.

Two things we tried on a limited basis this year and plan to continue and extend next year are home visits just before school starts and videotaped portfolios. The home visit is a scheduled, brief visit for the purpose of getting acquainted and taking a picture of the child at home. The videotape begins with five-year-olds talking about themselves early in the year and reading or telling a story later in the year. Two or three times a year each student will be videotaped as he or she is engaged in various activities and performances. This film may be used as an incentive to increase parent attendance at end-of-the-year conferences. It also is an excellent way to show personal growth over time.

We feel good about our new focus on assessment. Because of this focus, we study children to see how they learn so we can design a child-centered curriculum based on the continuous progress of each child. In the future, we will continue to fine-tune our assessment skills and strategies.

■ VISIONS FOR THE FUTURE

Next year there are several things we'd like to incorporate into our current program:

- We will work more closely with our upper primary family partners to develop opportunities for a wider age span and range of developmental abilities.

- We feel a need to learn more about the varied assessment tasks and rubrics we use, including both their implementation and development. (See Appendix A for our list of assessment tasks and tools and Appendix B for the rubric.)

- We will create our own developmental scales for emergent and continuing literacy (reading, writing, and math) based on what we see our children doing.

- We will make our 5" × 7" anecdotal record cards more "user friendly" by developing a list of child behaviors that indicate specific learning strategies common in young children. This would save valuable time. Instead of writing every specific behavior in narrative form each time we observe it, we could check it off on the record card and write the context.

We also hope the Kentucky Early Learning Profile (KELP), which will be in the field study stage in 1993–1994, will help make recording assessment information simpler and more consistent.

Although we have learned much from our struggle to develop our own assessment system, we feel it is important for all teachers to share a common perspective and philosophy. KERA's seven critical attributes, which include multi-age/multi-ability groupings, authentic assessment, and continuous progress, must be embraced as a *philosophy,* not as a prescription. In the new climate of reform, schools must meet the needs of children instead of trying to make children meet the requirements of school.

REFERENCES

Clay, M. M. (1975). *What Did I Write?* Aukland, New Zealand: Heinemann.

Goodman, Y. (1985). Kidwatching: Observing children in the classroom. In A. Jagger & M. T. Smith-Burke (Eds.), *Observing the Language Learner.* Newark, DE: International Reading Association.

Sulzby, E. (1985). Children's emergent reading of favorite storybooks: A developmental study. *Reading Research Quarterly, 20,* 458–481.

Sulzby, E. (1992). Transitions from emergent to conventional writing. *Language Arts, 69,* 290–297.

APPENDIX A

INFORMAL AND FORMAL ASSESSMENT DEVICES

INFORMAL	FORMAL
Anecdotal records	Developmental scales
Conferences	Individual learning goals
Sharing time	Checklists of basic skills/concepts
Peer questioning	Portfolios
Writing journals	Progress reports
Reading logs	KELP
Work samples	Performance tasks
Home visits	Performance rubrics
Video portfolio	Reading/Math assessment devices (e.g., M. Clay's The Early Detection of Reading Difficulties; NCTM's Mathematics for Young Children)

Appendix B

KENTUCKY LEARNING GOALS	LEARNER OUTCOMES	TASK NOT APPLICABLE	NOT OBSERVED	EMERGENT	DEVELOPING	ACCOMPLISHED	OUTSTANDING
GOAL 1 APPLYING BASIC SKILLS	Finding and Gathering Information and Ideas	N/A	NOT OBSERVED	relies on direction to identify and use source, tools, and skills to collect information and ideas with limited accuracy	is learning how to identify and use source, tools and skills to collect information and ideas with some meaning, reading, listening, etc.)	identifies and accurately uses source, tools and skills to collect information and ideas (e.g. meaning, reading, listening, etc.)	selects and fluently uses the most appropriate sources, tools and skills to collect information and ideas
	Organizing and Manipulating Information and Ideas	N/A	NOT OBSERVED	is beginning to sort, classify, and display information and ideas simply with limited accuracy	sorts, classifies, and displays information and ideas through a variety of concrete representations with some inaccuracies	sorts, classifies and displays information and ideas accurately through pictures, symbols and / or words	sorts, classifies and displays information and ideas in a fluent way showing patterns and complex relationships
	Expressing Information, Ideas, and Emotions	N/A	NOT OBSERVED	is beginning to express a basic ability to use written, oral, quantitative, physical, musical or artistic modes of expression	demonstrates increasing ability to use written, oral, quantitative, physical, musical or artistic modes of expression to convey meaning	can potentially demonstrate an ability to use written, oral, quantitative, physical, musical, or artistic modes of expression to convey meaning	demonstrates an exceptional ability to use written, oral, quantitative, physical, musical, or artistic modes of expression to convey meaning
GOAL 2 CONCEPTS	Conceptual Understanding	N/A	NOT OBSERVED	is starting to explore core concepts and principles	shows partial understanding of core concepts and principles	applies core concepts and principles to convey meaning	applies core concepts and principles deeply and broadly
GOAL 3 SELF-SUFFICIENCY	Task Commitment	N/A	NOT OBSERVED	was dependent upon assistance to complete task	completed task with some assistance	completed task/project independently with little or no assistance	persevered to fully complete project in a self-directed manner demonstrating ownership of the learning
	Self-Concept	N/A	NOT OBSERVED	beginning to have an awareness of own personal characteristics	recognizes own personal characteristics, possibly with some lack of acceptance; attempts to elicit humor through various forms of expression	describes/reveals self in a positive, realistic manner; consistently uses humor as a way to convey feelings of self in a positive way	describes/reveals self in positive relationship to others; exhibits a keen sense of humor and/or uses humor to explain complex relationship
GOAL 4 TEAM MEMBER	Cooperation	N/A	NOT OBSERVED	is beginning to learn how to work with others	works well in pairs, but with limited success in larger team situations	works consistently as a contributing member of team	works consistently and effectively as a contributing team member in a variety of roles
	Broadened Perspectives	N/A	NOT OBSERVED	is beginning to express awareness of the rights and responsibilities of self and others	recognizes the rights and responsibilities of self and others; recognizes different points of view	respects the rights and responsibilities of self and others; respects different points of view	respects the rights and responsibilities of self and others and advocates fairness; seeks out different points of view
GOAL 5 PROBLEM SOLVING	Strategies	N/A	NOT OBSERVED	is learning to use methods for solving problems	uses simple but reasonable methods for solving problems	uses multiple steps with workable methods for solving problems	decides upon most appropriate methods for solving problems by applying specific criteria
	Reasoning	N/A	NOT OBSERVED	is learning to give reasons for ideas	describes ideas with logic and evidence	explains ideas with sound logic and supporting evidence	explains ideas with sound logic and supporting evidence, making inferences, interpretations or conclusions
	Creativity	N/A	NOT OBSERVED	is able to retell or recreate familiar ideas with some assistance	is able to add new details or elaborate on a familiar concept with minimal assistance	invents unique methods and products to meet given conditions	invents unique methods and products using imagination to go beyond given limits
GOAL 6 INTEGRATION	Connections	N/A	NOT OBSERVED	is becoming aware of common ideas in various learning activities; is becoming aware of how to relate classroom learning and life experiences to each other	recognizes common ideas in various learning activities; recognizes situations where classroom learning and life experiences relate to each other	integrates two or more disciplines in learning activities; links classroom learning and life experiences to each other	focused learning on themes; develops "what if" questions linking classroom learning and life experiences to each other
	Learning How to Learn	N/A	NOT OBSERVED	is beginning to pose questions	poses questions to acquire new knowledge	constructs new understanding through investigation and inquiry	constructs, extends, interprets and applies new understandings through original research

PROJECT DISCOVERY
PRIMARY PORTFOLIO TALENT GUIDE PERFORMANCE TASK ASSESSMENT
Ohio Valley Educational Cooperative, LaGrange, KY 40031

Funded through a Grant for the United States Department of Education, Jacob K. Javits Gifted and Talented Students Education Prog

"LET THE WILD RUMPUS START!"*: THE STORY OF ONE MULTI-AGE/MULTI-ABILITY CLASSROOM

BY TINA CRON, JOY SPEARS, DONNA STOTTMANN
J.B. Atkinson Elementary Jefferson County Public Schools

C H 6 A P T E R

In the spring of 1991, three teachers decided to form a primary multi-age/multi-ability team. Donna joined Tina, knowing they shared similar philosophies. In discussions with their principal they found that Joy, the special education teacher, also had similar goals. As the three teachers sat together envisioning the multi-age classroom they would create, their goals were simple: (1) Children would be engaged in a learning environment where risk taking and decision making were the rule, and (2) the teachers would truly be a team, supporting each other's risk taking and growing together professionally. As they worked together, they began to realize that these goals could be achieved. And so, like Max in Sendak's *Where the Wild Things Are,* they boldly declared, "Let the wild rumpus start!"

◾ "SAIL IN AND OUT AND THROUGH A DAY" WITH US

7:45 A.M. Tina, a primary teacher at J. B. Atkinson Elementary, heads toward school. Loaded in her car are books on the environment that she has checked out from the public library. Donna, Tina's co-teacher, has already made her way to the Portland neighborhood in Louisville, where J. B. Atkinson is located. As she nears the school she notices the well-groomed lawn of one home that is in stark contrast to its neighbor, which is in serious disrepair.

* Sendak, M. (1963). *Where the Wild Things Are.* New York: Harper & Row.

8:00 A.M. On her way to the school Joy notices a billboard on one of the many corner bars in the area. The billboard proclaims, "There's Nothing Typical About It." Joy thinks to herself that the message could describe their neighborhood school with its wide array of families, children, teachers, and staff.

8:05 A.M. As Joy turns into the neighborhood, she waves to Jane, a seven-year-old, who is walking to school like most of the students at J. B. Atkinson. Jane and her mother join Ranee, an eight-year-old, as they walk into the building for breakfast. On Donna's way to the double-sized classroom she talks to a school psychologist who has tested Joe, a six-year-old, for a learning disability. Joy will add him to her class list of fifteen if his tests indicate that he has a learning disability.

8:15 A.M. As Donna enters, she glances at the mailboxes in the back of the room. She quickly pulls the name tag of Lakeisha, who has moved, off one box and replaces it with a tag for Temecia, the newest member of the team. She counts more than ten changes to the mailboxes this year and hopes that the class will not change again for the last two months of school.

Minutes before the children arrive, the teachers share highlights of the weekend. They scurry around the room gathering and organizing materials for the introduction of their unit on the rain forest. Many books are arranged around the room. Donna searches frantically for additional copies of the book *Rainforest Secrets,* and Tina thinks through a lesson on animals from *The Great Kapok Tree.* They briefly share what they have each learned about rain forests since Friday's planning session and review how to begin the unit so as to captivate the children from the very first lesson.

8:45 A.M. The class, otherwise known as the Ladybugs, arrives with stories about the weekend, and children begin to write in their journals. Jessica copies words she can find around the room, and Clarence describes the weekend he spent with his dad. Joy reminds Joey to leave space between his words. Tina encourages a reluctant Marquis to share his writing about Ninja Turtles, his topic for the past five months. He shyly declines to share, but Jaquain, another six-year-old, leans over and offers to read aloud for him. Sharing continues, followed by a song as the journals go back into their baskets.

9:30 A.M. "Story Groups" gather with each of the three teachers for reading and writing minilessons. A low hum comes from one side of the room as Donna and a group of eight- and nine-year-olds search for information on animal and plant life in the rain forests. They read to each other and comment on the things they find particularly interesting. A discussion ensues about animals that have peculiar looks, and the children share what they already know about animals of the rain forest. One or two sneak a peek at another group to whom Joy is reading aloud. She follows with a lesson on using context clues to identify unknown words. Down the hall in a half room, Tina uses animals of the rain forest to teach a small group lesson on the food chain to emergent readers.

10:10 A.M. As the two groups rejoin the rest of the class, they gather their writing folders and listen to new writing choices and suggestions. As the writing time begins, Jodi, a self-motivated learner, takes a text she wants to publish and begins typing. A small group has chosen to gather around Donna to work on a rain forest dictionary. DeShaun, Mekale, and Marquis, all six-year-olds, find each other to continue co-authoring a book about basketball. Their goal is to have the piece published in time for the next authoring party, a monthly event. Khrys takes dictation from DeMar, a frustrated writer. Joe, an emergent writer, starts and finishes a wordless picture book and spends the next twenty minutes asking others to listen while he "reads" his book. Some offer suggestions for change, which he declines. DeMont, an experienced writer with a learning disability, conferences with Brad in an effort to correct his spelling.

10:50 A.M. Bob finally locates his writing folder beneath the computer table. It is apparent that he will have nothing to share today and will need specific directions tomorrow.

11:00 A.M. Students share what they have written in a whole-class setting. Some tell of frustrations they have had, and others describe plans for tomorrow's work time. For example, RaShawn eagerly shares the story draft he has been working on for three days, but he wants help on his ending. Tina asks the whole group for suggestions in order to give RaShawn ideas and to support what he has already completed. Cindy suggests that he keep the rhyming pattern; Justin says that he likes that the characters are animals and tells him to draw the ending. Tina suggests that he take Justin's advice and offers to help him tomorrow if he is still stuck.

<u>11:45 A.M.</u> After the children have finished lunch, the rainy day sends them to recess stations in the room. Activity choices include: Lincoln logs, Legos, play dough, chalkboards, listening station, puppets, and board games. Jaquain makes his daily board game choice of "Sorry." He is learning to take his turn and follow the rules of the game. Brad joins him and uses strategies he has learned to outwit the others. Sam is catching on to Brad's moves and challenges him. A group of girls plays school, each child taking a turn as teacher. The younger girls write color words while the older ones teach from their pretend "Box It, Bag It" calendar. After thirty minutes, Tina starts the Ladybug team song, and the children take that as a cue to start cleaning up their areas. By the end of the song most are back in their seats and ready for Theme Time.

<u>12:15 P.M.</u> Theme Time drives the curriculum. It is a time to teach science and social studies content by engaging the students in experiments, writing activities, partner discovery time, and direct teaching. Tina starts by discussing parts of the rain forest, and students try to guess where ten animals live. Tina's story group, mostly six- and seven-year-olds, have a lot to contribute. They bring prior knowledge from their morning lesson. After a minilesson on food chains, partners turn to each other and begin constructing their own model of the food chain. Each pair has been grouped to complement the partners' strengths and offset their weaknesses. The noise level rises as coloring, cutting, and gluing take place. Khrys reminds Joey to stay at the table as she gathers supplies. Different ages and developmental levels produce diverse discussions. Bruce and Ranee disagree about one animal's quickness in relation to its size. Javon and Mekale decide they would like to be jaguars at the top of the food chain. As the teachers monitor group work, they have different expectations for each child. For example, Mekale, a six-year-old, might be expected to make connections with stories that are read aloud, while Javon, an eight-year-old, is expected to analyze and evaluate information. After closing and sharing as a whole group, the children tuck their products into theme time folders and return

these to the baskets on the shelf just in time to line up for art, music, library, or physical education.

1:15 P.M. Planning time begins as the teachers prepare materials for mathematics, and Donna asks for suggestions on the math lesson she has planned for the day. They talk about Alan's need for some one-on-one teaching with fractions and about math journal entries. The conversation follows its usual path, jumping from topic to topic until it is time to pick up the children. The three teachers go in different directions, leaving loose ends to be tied up later.

1:45 P.M. DEAR (Drop Everything and Read) time allows the children to interact with the books of their choice. Clarence gets his chapter book from his mailbox and rounds up the others who have chosen the same book, as Steve flips through the baskets of trade books looking for an old favorite. Justin invites Megan to sit on the floor by his table to read *Five Little Monkeys Jumping on the Bed.* They crowd on top of the big book while two others leaning from their chairs chime in on their favorite parts. Sara, a very fluent nine-year-old reader, goes to the rocking chair, where she loses herself in a novel. Tina circulates, encouraging the children to use softer voices. Donna listens as Mandy reads aloud from *J.T.* to the group that has gathered to tackle this chapter book.

When the timer goes off, most of the children move to find a reading partner. Brad, an eight-year-old, reads aloud Brown's *Arthur's Loose Tooth* to Tim, a six-year-old and a captive audience. They talk about the pictures, and Tim benefits from the one-on-one interaction Brad is able to provide. Reading with Tim allows Brad time to practice voice inflection and fluency without the risk of criticism. Upon completion of the story, Tim jumps up, ready to dash to the bookshelf. Brad, who has already internalized the routine and knows Tim's tendency to wander, gently says, "You stay here, Tim, and I'll get another book because you know you sometimes have trouble remembering to come back." Joy wraps up DEAR time by reading aloud from the group novel, Sachar's *Sideways Stories from Wayside School.*

2:15 P.M. Joy calls her math group to line up for the computer lab. They have a lesson that supports the previous day's instruction on

regrouping. Tina and Donna instruct their group to get their math folders. Each folder contains a week's worth of math projects to complete at each of the nine centers. Assignments vary per child. These centers include: weighing, patterns, estimating, graphing, computation, a counting chart, problem solving, calculators, and unifix cubes. The teachers use these same stations or centers for each theme, adapting the activities for the theme and for specific children. For example, the graphing activity involves coloring and graphing the child's favorite rain forest animal. James is working with a calculator to complete his computation worksheets. He talks to Kelly while they work. Kelly sees that James's answer does not match hers and says, "Oh, look! You made a mistake. You pushed a 6; it's a 9" as she points to a button on the calculator.

At the weighing station Tina works with three students weighing plastic bear counters. She explains how the weights can balance the pan of bears and that by adding the weights one can discover how much the bears weigh. This new concept will be teacher directed for the first week.

Andy and Tim are working at the measuring station. Each has a large plastic box of rice and several measuring cups. The task is a follow-up to a directed lesson. Tim holds the 1/2 cup and Andy tries to figure out how many 1/4's will fill the 1/2 cup. Joe is working at the 100's chart to color in the numbers one says when counting by 5's. He has trouble with the counting and asks Jane for help. She slowly counts aloud, and he colors each number she says. Then, seeing the pattern, he exclaims, "I get it—it's all the numbers that end in 5 and 0."

Meanwhile, at the estimating center, two children estimate M&M's, marshmallows, and beans in separate jars of different sizes. Ken studies the jar of M&M's. He says, "I think there are nine" and writes his guess by the picture of the M&M jar on his worksheet.

Later, Tina invites all the children finished with their work to sit on the floor with her and find out if their estimates of the M&M's, beans, and marshmallows were close to the actual number. She has all the children report their estimates and tell how they came up with their guesses. Most responses are like Ken's. He says, "I just guessed in my head." Tina counts the M&M's in groups of ten and periodically stops and asks, "How many so far?" The children count in chorus, "Ten, twenty, thirty, forty." Tina says, "OK, we have four groups of ten, how many is that? Then five more, forty-one, forty-two, forty-three, forty-four, forty-five." Then she looks at the recording sheet and examines the children's estimates. She tells the children how many M&M's are in the jar and asks the children which estimate is closest to the actual number. Jaquain is closest; he is asked to tell how he came up with his estimate. He says, "I just thought of it." Tina asks, "Well, why didn't you guess 100?" He says, "Because 100 would be too big." She asks, "But why didn't you guess two?" He says, "'Cause it's [the jar and candy] too big for two." Tina nods and says, "Thirty-one is a good guess." She moves on to count the marshmallows and puts them in groups of two. She gets the kids to count with her. Halfway through counting, she asks if any want to revise their estimates; several do. They finish putting them in groups of two and count them together for a total of fifteen. She asks which child made the best guess. They say Justin, and she asks him how he came up with the estimate. He says, "They were big enough to count." Tina says, "When there are only a few you can try counting them and then guess." Then they move on to the beans. A bunch of children revise their estimates even before she begins. When Tina asks why, their answers reflect their knowledge of the estimates of the candy and marshmallows.

Some children have their own agenda at times and use materials to experiment. At the unifix cubes, Megan has connected many cubes that are in a pattern (the instructions at the station) but is using them to measure Laquita's back.

For the last ten minutes the group comes together on the floor to share what they've learned. Donna leads the discussion while Tina makes a note to herself that none of the children can share about problem solving because they can't read the worksheet. She also decides that she will have to choose Laquita's centers tomorrow because Laquita was unproductive today. Before the folders are put away, each child tells Donna what his or her first station will be tomorrow.

3:15 P.M. As the day closes, the groups go to their mailboxes to collect homework assignments. David, a younger child, will label pictures of the rain forest animals, and Sally, an older child, will write a paragraph describing what would happen if one of the animals in the food chain became extinct. Joy and Donna ask trivia questions about the present and previous units of study while they wait for the afternoon announcements. Tina fills out three daily reports that go home and reminds those who are checking out classroom books to sign them out on the board. Donna and Joy share a surprised look when Jessica, a seven-year-old, beautifully answers her trivia question about animals from the Arctic region. She usually needs help from her eight-year-old partner. Megan, a competitive six-year-old, smiles proudly as she gives the answer to 100 multiplied by 5. The last ten minutes are a flurry of activity as buses are called and walkers shuffle out the door.

3:25 P.M. In a quiet room, all three teachers take a deep breath to unwind as they wait for their second wind. Tina shares tidbits about her math lesson and concerns about Leigh Ann's progress. Joy reminds the others about the meeting the following day to review Andy's annual learning goals and gets input from them regarding his work in their groups. Plans are made for a small group minilesson during tomorrow's writing work time for several students who are ready to start using the dictionary independently. Some individual time is spent reflecting on the day and thinking ahead to tomorrow. Tina, Joy, and Donna leave the building knowing that it has been a productive day.

■ "IN AND OUT OF WEEKS AND OVER TWO YEARS": OUR JOURNEY

Fall, 1991. Three university textbooks on emergent literacy are open on Donna's plan book, which has erasures and sticky notes all over it. A pile of interim progress reports peeks out from under a stack of unexamined homework papers, and three phone messages, still unreturned, glare at her from amidst the mess. Glancing around at Tina's and Joy's desks, one finds similar confusion. Library books and teacher resource books are strewn among assessment labels and pieces of broken crayons. Where were we finding the energy to spend almost twelve hours a day working to make our team successful? Arriving early and planning late were only part of our day's activities when we were not teaching. We were practically joined at the hip discussing samples of students' work, debating the merits of a schedule change, or thinking aloud a lesson to ensure that we were meeting all the children's needs. We spent evenings reading about early childhood development and researching our latest thematic unit. We were committed from the start as we watched the group of children we had in our room begin to feel comfortable taking risks.

Although we all had similar philosophies about whole language and hands-on experiences, we had varying degrees of expertise in working with primary-aged children. We constantly second-guessed our gut feelings about appropriate material, and we were uncertain that the children were learning what they should be, especially the six-year-olds.

We spent hours planning and trying to understand development, yet we were not sure that the book making, oral reading, science experiments, cooperative learning activities, and problem solving were going to produce the quality thinkers, readers, and writers we expected. Throughout the year we were given the freedom to design our own curriculum, and although it was quite an exhausting endeavor, at the same time it proved to be energizing. Working around thematic units exposed the children to literature, writing projects, science projects, drama, and art in a related way. In the early part of the year much of our planning time was spent discussing curriculum and gathering resources.

Our planning paid off. The multi-age concept seemed to be working. Our older students acted as scribes for the younger ones, and these joint efforts produced wonderful class books. The exceptional-education students who lacked confidence and skills felt safe reading titles like *Are You My Mother?* over and over to their younger partners or group mates. Multi-aged reading and writing groups studied predictable books in the early part of the year and produced puppets and learning dialogue for *Jump Frog Jump.* The youngest readers may have mis-sequenced who chased whom, but all of them chimed in on, "How did the frog get away? Jump Frog Jump!" This book remained a class favorite throughout the year. The emergent readers continued to retell the story by "reading the pictures" and delighted in the AHA! experience of one-to-one correspondence between text and what they read as their sight word vocabulary grew.

By December we realized that we could not do it all. Our families were beginning to have trouble recognizing us, and we began to finish each other's thoughts. We had been spending time working on structural aspects of the program. We were forever trying to come up with a suitable room arrangement that allowed for the movement we wanted as well as common space for whole group lessons. The schedule needed adjusting, and we analyzed almost everything everyone did and said, including the lessons we taught and the books we read. To keep ourselves from becoming overwhelmed, we began delegating lessons to teach rather than planning everything together, and we took turns completing paperwork and parent correspondence.

After the January winter break we started with a bang. We were geared up and ready to go with an abundance of resources for our dinosaur unit. It was at the conclusion of this unit that we allowed ourselves to step back and reflect. In doing so, we were able to see the tremendous growth that had been made, and our goals for each child became more individualized. The team spirit we had fostered from the beginning was blending nicely with the social skills the children had acquired. The children had come to know each other, and the cooperative climate was an underlying strength we could not have done without. Until this point in the year we had accepted everything and applauded risk taking.

We also realized in January that the more experienced learners were ready for more challenges. Laticia, a student who was not as internally motivated as some, was required to show more evidence of what she could do. We led her away from predictable books and nudged her into reading more complex texts. She chose to join the group reading Kimmel's *Chocolate Fever,* and we delighted in her newfound area of leadership in the world of chapter books. We also delighted in our own success. We were feeling comfortable with our curriculum choices and developmentally appropriate lessons as well as with our kid-watching techniques. However, our struggle with assessment and student expectations was rising to the surface.

We had many questions about how to document progress and share the huge number of notes we had written about the children. We had been piloting a primary report card that no longer used traditional letter grades. It was designed to compare a child with him- or herself by focusing on process rather than product. Our reporting methods seemed very subjective, and we were used to having a grading system. It was our initial intention to write a narrative report on each child and use videotaped interviews and writing samples over time to show academic growth. The reality of this thinking became an issue of time and space. There were not enough hours in the day to write about the connections and insights the students had and to make notes about their interviews.

"What *should* a child know at the end of each year in the primary program?" was the ever-present question. We struggled with ways to communicate about progress with administrators, parents, and even the students. There was no one to tell us what "rapid progress" or "steady progress" meant or if rapid and steady could differ for different children. We also knew that others were asking similar questions, and there did not seem to be a "final word" anywhere. It was a process all piloting schools were going through. We continued to plunge through the remainder of the year discussing, reading, and trying to make our own professional judgments about assessment.

As May drew to a close, we had some definite ideas about the merits of the multi-aged/multi-ability program we had developed. This mandated KERA program had professionally challenged us as learners ourselves, and we valued our new insights and reflections. It was time to begin addressing the questions that had remained unanswered as we finished out one year and set our sights on the next.

Fall, 1992. Planning and decision making moved much more efficiently. We knew that our curriculum would be cyclical and had decided on schoolwide themes to alleviate some of the problems with resources. We spent supply money on resources to support our curriculum. We made very few changes in our program at the start of the year and anticipated the children's return with similar plans for team building and cooperative lessons. We agreed that we would continue some ability grouping for math where necessary and that our whole language classroom would continue to evolve with the children. The schedule was changed, but we started the school year with enthusiasm and confidence. It was in October that we began to feel frustrated and exhausted.

We wanted the children to be more self-sufficient and to be making decisions about what they wanted to learn. We felt that the schedule changes broke the familiar and comfortable routines and that we had different concerns about our eight-year-olds than we had been faced with in the previous year.

It was on a Sunday afternoon at Tina's house that we began to share some of our wishes and set some new goals. It seemed that we were trying to make circles fit into square holes. The children seemed resistant to the new schedule we had created and, keeping them in mind, we went back to the drawing board. We wanted to have a small block of time just to teach reading strategies. Some of the older children had very different needs than the emergent readers. They needed some time devoted completely to their literacy needs. Joy wanted some concentrated time with her exceptional education students, many of whom were new to our team, and she needed to focus on their specific needs. Tina agreed to take the emergent readers and expose them to material appropriate for their development. We also felt a strong need to integrate all three age groups for an extended period of reading and writing that we termed "work time." It was our goal to have this block of the day be student directed and to allow for as many of the seven intelligences (Gardner & Hatch, 1990) as possible. It proved to be one of our most valuable moves. Work time is our most effective multi-aged/multi-ability period.

After we made these major schedule adjustments, the pieces of the puzzle began to fit. Days turned to weeks, and weeks to months, and then it was finally the close of our second year as primary teachers. We had continued to follow the children's lead. We made adjustments to meet their needs and interests. We valued their decision-making abilities and their insights. We talked often of our progress as well as theirs. In a districtwide inservice in the summer of 1991, Pat Todd, director of restructuring for Jefferson County Schools, spoke of the primary program, comparing it with a family vacation. She pointed out that families go together but that each member brings back something different from the experience. For our team of teachers and students, it has not all been a vacation. However, given the chance to buy the same ticket again, we wouldn't even need the supersaver to entice us.

■ IT'S NOT TERRIBLE ROARS AND GNASHING OF TERRIBLE TEETH: ADVANTAGES TO THE MULTI-AGED CLASSROOM

Advantages are plentiful in a multi-age setting. We chose to discuss the few that impact us the most. First, having children for three to four years instead of only one year enables us to watch them blossom from year to year and to spend less time at the beginning of the school year getting to know each child. We already know their strengths and weaknesses. The very first day of this school year we expected Brad to write lengthy journal entries and Bob, his frequent partner, to use beginning and ending sounds when spelling. Thus, the first day felt less like a "first day of school" and more like a reunion. Tracking a student's success for two years has provided us with well-rounded views of our students, who get the added comfort and sense of stability from well-known adults. Our students' parents feel the same way about these advantages. They develop a closer relationship with us from year to year. It is also easier for them to reflect upon their child's success in their primary years with us there to help.

In our classroom, we daily make decisions about developmentally appropriate lessons for each age range. Having such a wide age range from the outset forces us to provide a curriculum that is developmentally appropriate for six-, seven-, eight-, and nine-year-olds as well as for children with learning disabilities. We now make more provisions for all learning abilities, which is a great advantage for all of our students. Our varied curriculum also allows our exceptional education students to find their niche and feel good about themselves in a regular classroom. Our second-year students with learning disabilities do not know they have been identified as having learning disabilities. For example, Bob, one of our more active second-year students, has feelings of insecurity. He depends on us for daily compliments and moral support to get through the day successfully. Last year Bob was tested for reading and writing disabilities and at the end of May was designated as an exceptional education student. This year he was simply added to Joy's roll. He only knows that often he gets to work with Joy during story group time and that Joy loves to read his stories. Had Bob been in a traditional second grade classroom and pulled out to work with a special teacher, his self-esteem probably would have plummeted. In our exceptional-education collaborative room, he is still a leader and just a regular child. Having these students full-time also means that students and parents do not stigmatize Joy as the special education teacher.

Having Joy on the team benefits not only the children but also Donna and Tina. When the teachers decided to collaborate in the Spring of 1991, no one envisioned how great the moral and physical support would be for the team of teachers. They depend on each other every day while collaborating on both planning and teaching lessons. During Tina's recent lesson on insects, Donna sat in as a group member and interacted with the students. Joy circulated to keep stragglers on task, passed out supplies, and drifted past a few students to remind them of strategies they could use.

Teaming provides the opportunity to divide the students into smaller groups for more directed teaching. This is a time for students to get extra one-on-one time with a teacher as well as experience working in a small group. Teaming also provides the chance for teachers to learn from one another. Each teacher has an area of expertise that fosters collaboration. Donna provides insight on the nature of cooperative learning; Joy reminds us to focus on the needs of the individual learner and to provide them strategies to succeed; and Tina develops ways to enhance positive behavior in our room. This relationship allows teachers to focus on and become experts in a few areas and depend on others for support in weaker areas. Our experience and education are very different, but each teacher feels important, needed, and valued.

■ AND OUR SUPPER IS STILL HOT: REFLECTIONS

Our experience with the primary program is both a struggle and a joy. It provides us with challenges and victories as the children grow. Each time we see Brad explain a concept to Kelly we believe more strongly in the primary program. Each time Megan imitates the oral reading inflections of Sara we know we are on the right path. Each time Andy, an exceptional-education student, raises his hand confidently to share a piece of writing, we are reminded of the responsibility of fostering success. Just as teachers with different experiences and areas of expertise are able to work together, we learn that children of different ages and abilities can work together. Simply put, our goal is to allow all to benefit from each other. As Bruce, an eight-year-old, said of his tablemate, Justin, a six-year-old, "He is one of the best teachers I have ever had!"

REFERENCES

Gardner, H., & Hatch, T. (1990). Multiple intelligences go to school: Educational implications of the theory of multiple intelligences. *Educational Researcher, 18,* 4–10.

MULTI-AGE, MULTI-*ABILITIES*: AN INCLUSIVE PRIMARY PROGRAM

BY PHILLIP POORE AND
CHERYL ARMSTRONG
Paxton Wilt Elementary
Jefferson County Schools

C H A P T E R

As twelve pairs of bright eyes and attentive ears soaked up an oral reading of the *True Story of the Three Little Pigs*, four pairs of busy hands created a large story map of *Rosie's Walk*, and ten active bodies prepared a dramatic performance of *Ten in a Bed*, two adult visitors entered our learning space once again. What they observed, upon entering, may have looked chaotic and disorganized, but in reality it was learning at its best—small-grouped, child-centered, and purposeful.

Our teaching assistant, Ms. Schnurr, was reading *The True Story of the Three Little Pigs* aloud to a group of students. This group had previously read and discussed a more traditional version of The Three Little Pigs and was preparing to make a Venn diagram to compare and contrast the two versions. In another area of the room, a group of five- and six-year-old students was working with Mr. Poore to demonstrate comprehension, map and directional skills, and measuring techniques by creating a map to depict where Rosie went on her walk. Having just finished reading *Ten in a Bed*, a group of six- and seven-year-olds was sequencing events of the story with Ms. Armstrong. Later they would present their dramatization of the story to the rest of the class.

The visitors present on this particular day were observing typical learning activities that occur in our primary school classroom. Our school employs forty full-time and eleven part-time staff members, and it has a student population of 395, 26 percent of whom are African American. It serves populations from two neighborhoods: one is a predominantly white population that lives in suburban apartment complexes and homes near the school, and the other is a predominantly African-American population residing in suburban apartment complexes and homes approximately six miles from the school. The socioeconomic level of both populations can be described as low to moderate.

Our classroom generally serves twenty-seven six-, seven-, and eight-year-old students, four of whom have been identified as multiple handicapped. The multiple-handicapped students have low cognitive skills and are handicapped in at least one other area that affects their learning. Three of the multiple-handicapped students are eight years old; one is nine. All of them are extremely developmentally delayed, have very short attention spans, and suffer from poor self-esteem. Ben exhibits "autistic" behaviors and has limited language skills. Another student, Megan, has fetal alcohol syndrome, which causes her to have visual problems and poor fine-motor skills. Bobby transferred to our program from a combination learning disability/behavior disorder self-contained class. When he first arrived, he interacted angrily and aggressively with both adults and other students. The fourth student is John, who has poor fine-motor skills, and he too, struggles with academic work. None of these four students has experienced success in their previous years in school.

■ ■ ■ ■ ■ ■ ■ ■ ■ ■ ■

The twenty-seven students in this classroom receive guidance, support, and instruction from a variety of adults. Phil Poore is the regular program teacher, and Cheryl Armstrong is the collaborating special education teacher. Cheryl divides each day between this classroom and another primary classroom. Throughout any given day, two or three other instructional assistants work to help all students progress. This team of adults works to create an inclusive classroom where all students are challenged and guided to meet their potential.

Each day math-concept teaching is conducted during a morning time block from 9:15 to 10:30. Generally between 10:30 and 12:00 students are engaged in shared reading, author studies, sustained silent reading, poetry reading, and writing workshop. After lunch we set aside a large block of time to teach science and social studies concepts within a year-long study of communities. During this time we also integrate reading, writing, and math minilessons as appropriate.

Our visitors for that day were a parent of a student being placed in the multiple-handicapped (MH) class and the counselor from the student's previous school. Their purpose for being there was to assess the appropriateness of this placement. After they had observed for a while, we asked the visitors if they could identify who the special needs students were. They could not, guessing at three regular program students. This inability to identify the special needs students is not unusual in our classroom. At times even the administrators and other teachers cannot identify the students labeled as being handicapped in some way or as having special needs. This fact points to the underlying reason for creating multi-age, multi-ability classes and especially for integrating special needs students into those classes. *It eliminates the labeling so often associated with failure.* Our particular philosophy of inclusion and acceptance is what we feel makes our program most successful.

■ OUR PHILOSOPHY OF INCLUSION

We share the philosophy that all children learn best when given the opportunity to work with others of varying ability levels. We want our students to have the perspective that any given group is composed of individuals with unique talents and skills. This is how it is in the real world, and we want that reflected in our classroom.

We both formulated this philosophy during our special education training. As special education teachers we learned to teach to multi-age, multi-ability groups of students. We assessed needs and developed programs to meet those needs. We ascertained student learning styles, developmental levels, and environmental influences that affect learning. In other words, we sought to teach the whole child. The flaw was that we were trying to achieve this in a self-contained classroom where all students were labeled as having special needs. Today we seek to apply our belief in teaching all children holistically to a regular classroom setting. Our primary school format provides the vehicle through which we can achieve that goal.

In reflecting on how well we have implemented our philosophy in the daily instruction of our students, we find many successes and some areas that still need work. Our ability to collaborate and our support staff provide the backbone of the success. We plan together, communicate student progress, discuss strategies, and evaluate instructional methods. Each of us is able and willing to work with any student or any group at a given time. We have developed flexibility in setting and altering schedules as needed. In our program, we can't be hung up on time. The special education teacher or her assistant is always present, and they especially make sure that the special needs students receive the individual attention and services as outlined in their Individualized Educational Plans (IEPs).

Administrative support also ensures success in that the teachers are encouraged to act as decision makers in determining what's best for each child. It has helped educate and inform parents of the benefits of inclusive teaching. We have found that parent support is essential to achieving our goals.

At the beginning of the year, the students often identified each other by their differences. But because of our attitude of acceptance, by the end of the year they were more likely to view each other as team-mates with many similarities.

■ EMPOWERING STUDENTS BY OFFERING CHOICES

Another essential element of our program is that we provide a safe environment that enables the students to make choices involving their own learning. This respect for students' ideas and feelings empowers the students to initiate their own learning and cultivate a respect for others in the room. We provide the safety for ideas, reinforce progress, and allow students to make mistakes and self-evaluate those mistakes. The following questions are often heard in our classroom: "How would you like to show what you learned?" "Who would you like to work with?" "What materials would you like to use?" "What do you think you did well on that project?" "What did you learn when you did this?" "What could you do to improve?" "How could you make this better?"

To illustrate how student choices are interwoven into the fabric of the instruction, we include this excerpt from Mr. Poore's journal:

Today the students voted to read the big book version of The Doorbell Rang by Pat Hutchins. I read it aloud to the whole group first just for enjoyment. After the second reading, the students and I talked about what they could learn from the story. The kids were able to discover some learnings such as addition (adding people who came over), dividing the cookies among a group of people, and subtracting cookies. Some students talked about fractions being used. For example, if they were dividing cookies, they might have to cut them into portions in order to share them equally. Because the students seemed so interested in the concept, I taught a basic lesson about fractions later in the day. It was successful!

At the end of the book, we talked about why the little boy decid-ed to open the door and let in more people. The kids figured out that he had seen Grandma through the door holding cookies. We also talked about why that was a good decision. We talked about what would have been on the other side of the door to make that a bad decision. They figured out that it would have been a bad decision if there had only been more kids and not more cookies.

After several readings with the kids reading along with me, I asked them what they could do to respond to this book in a written form. They were able to brainstorm ideas of ways to write about it. They suggested that they could write about their favorite part and illustrate it, retell the story in writing and illustrate, change the ending, and write an advertisement to convince someone to read the book.

After most of the students finished their writing pieces, we gathered on the rug to share with peers what they had written. Megan had drawn symbols to retell the story. She was able to interpret these symbols to the class in a way that showed she understood the plot and remembered the sequence. Ben located his favorite part in the book by pointing to the picture. Bobby shared how he would change the ending to the story and was able to draw an advertisement. John wrote a sentence about his favorite part and then acted it out, drawing upon his creativity. This sharing seems to validate their writing, gives them an audience, and encourages them to be creative and write for a purpose.

Another way we teach concepts while still giving students choices is through author studies. We have students choose an author of a book they especially like and then do a study of that author's other writing. We take several books by one author, read them over the course of several weeks, making the author and his or her writing style and subject matter the focus. Many skills, including comprehension, sequencing, open response, motivation techniques, comparing/contrasting, and character analysis, can be taught through this study. It is terrific when students can identify the author of a book because they are familiar with his or her style and typical subject matter. It also gives students such as Megan, whose writing skills are so minimal, an opportunity to participate successfully in critical analysis of literature. One of our favorite authors is Leo Lioni, who writes about imagination, community, and working together. We also like books by Eric Carle for his type of tissue paper illustrations, Steven Kellogg's Pinkerton series because the students love the dog, and Pat Hutchins for the simplicity and warmth in the story lines.

■ ACCOUNTABILITY IN WRITING INSTRUCTION

Someone asked us how we are accountable for writing skills. In our multi-age, multi-ability class, writing skills are individualized. When students write a response of any kind, they know they are to write to the fullest extent of their ability. Each individual's plan is based on where that person was the last time he or she wrote. For example, a special needs student may respond verbally while an assistant records his or her thoughts. Other students might be working on putting their thoughts on paper, learning to trust themselves to write the sounds they hear in the thoughts they have. They are practicing listening to their own voices, not spelling every word conventionally. Other students are putting words together to make sentences (complete thoughts) that make sense. Those who are adept at writing complete thoughts begin to capitalize and punctuate, and they see the benefit of knowing where one thought ends and another one begins. Capitalization and punctuation become useful only after the children are able to put complete thoughts on paper. Still other children work on combining sentences with a common idea to form paragraphs. They ask, "How do I let my reader know this is a new idea?" We tell them to indent the first line to show that a new idea is coming. At that point, those students see the benefit of knowing how to indent. Therefore, they are more likely to remember to use that knowledge.

This is also a time when Bobby may share his ideas with a general education student, and the two of them may write a piece together. The general education student initially does the actual writing, and Bobby will later tell the class about it.

■ USE OF POETRY TO TEACH READING/WRITING

Accountability for reading skills is handled during Sustained Silent Reading with individual conferences and when students are in skills groups for a short period. We use literature books and poetry during these group times. We use poetry a great deal because it provides a small chunk of reading that is more comfortable for many students to attack and grasp. They are not overwhelmed by length. We read poems that are humorous, serious, seasonal, theme-oriented, and fun. We use poems that are generally on the student's reading level. However, we do read more sophisticated poems to younger students and simple, silly ones to older students as well. We do not expect students who need to be reading less-sophisticated texts to read a very complex poem, and we don't usually use simple poems as instructional material for more accomplished readers. However, students across age levels enjoy listening to poetry of varying levels of reading difficulty. For example, Ben has difficulty reading and speaking, yet he can appreciate stories and poems read aloud to him. He can demonstrate this by telling what he likes about them.

We usually write poems on chart paper for all to see. The students hear the poems several times, discuss them, and read them together with the teacher. Then partners read together. After repeated readings, students are challenged to read the poems themselves. All the students have poetry notebooks in which they put their poems. We do not have students write their poems in the notebook, because the purpose here is not handwriting. Instead, we photocopy the poems, which they paste in their notebooks. They complete an illustration or write a reflection about particular poems to demonstrate some comprehension. In this manner, they can display their knowledge of characters, setting, problems, and solutions related to the poem. Because we want the poetry notebook to be a collection of material the students can read, we choose material based on their individual progress. We choose material that is challenging but not frustrating for their reading ability.

Usually, we ask the students what kinds of words they notice in a particular poem, what sounds seem to occur often, and what words they can understand from the context. Younger students may notice words that begin with similar sounds, rhyming words, or words with similar endings.

On one occasion a teachable-moment topic became compound words. We were reading a poem on chart paper and a six-year-old said, "There's a word that has two little words in it." She was asked to point out the word and to tell us what she meant. The word was *into*. She said, "Well, I see *in* and *to* and it's all put together and it's a word." The students were then able to find other compound words in that poem. In subsequent poems the students continued to identify compound words. As a result of one child noticing the compound word *into*, that group of students was sensitized to identifying compound words and explaining their meanings. We truly believe this sensitivity was created because a peer noticed the word and brought it to the other students' attention. It is possible they might have learned compound words from the teacher, but their fascination with them might not have been as great. We enjoyed watching the students become excited about compound words.

We believe that if students are given the opportunities to discover things themselves, great learning can occur. When they discover things on their own in an environment where they are free to explore, their learning is accentuated. We now seek opportunities to provide students with many different types of experiences. We want to spark their interest, motivate them to discover, and prompt them to ask questions to which they will find answers and solutions.

In another reading/writing activity, we read *The Cat in the Hat* by Dr. Seuss aloud to the whole group. Then we had the students work in groups to think of as many rhyming words as they could for *cat*. The students shared their lists with the entire class. Then we had them choose a word from their list with which to make a sentence. The only stipulation was that the word that rhymed with *cat* had to be the last word in the sentence. We wrote six of the students' sentences on the board. They noticed that two of the sentences were about the same topic and that three others were about a similar topic. We wrote the two sentences together and the three together and talked about how the two groups could be poems because the sentences were about the same topic and told a story. We discussed the rhyme in these poems but also noted that rhyme is not necessary in a poem.

Our idea was to continue this process of sentence making and have the groups create their own poems. Because we used cooperative groups for this activity, all the students were able to participate regardless of their instructional level. One group member was the recorder. Everyone in the group was a contributor. All were actively involved in making the list of rhyming words and creating the sentences.

Cooperative learning is a strategy that we use to facilitate student progress. It has enabled students of all abilities to be successful and to actively participate in their learning. It is a natural tool to use to create an atmosphere of acceptance of individual differences and learning styles and the opportunity for peer relationships. It is particularly helpful with the special needs students, who may be able to perform parts of the learning task but not all. They can participate verbally, encourage other group members, keep time, and illustrate.

■ MATH-CONCEPT TEACHING

In teaching mathematics, we focus on concept teaching and utilize whatever activities, manipulatives, and strategies that we decide will best serve that concept. Some of the sources from which we draw are *Box It, Bag It Math, Success in Understanding Mathematics, Math Their Way,* and the Scott, Foresman teacher material. We also provide math centers so students have a variety of hands-on experiences. Math manipulatives are always available at the centers so that students can experiment with math concepts, making discoveries on their own. Centers consist of unifix cubes with which students can build, create patterns, and work with group sets; geoboards and bands to allow students to experiment with shapes and designs; and pattern blocks with which they can be creative and discover how shapes work together. The centers provide many opportunities for the special needs students to experience success. They can handle the materials and attempt tasks with the aid of general-education partners. For example, Megan experimented with the weights of given objects using ceramic tiles. She was able to count how many tiles each object weighed and order the objects from lightest to heaviest. Ben paired with another student to create patterns. The other child originated the pattern while Ben created it. In this activity, each child was having his or her learning needs met.

Students also use magnetic manipulative pieces that stick to the chalkboard to bridge the links between the manipulative, picture, and abstract (signs and numbers) levels of math understanding. Students use color cubes to create three-dimensional figures from picture presentations. We like this to be a time that is not directed by us, but one when students use the materials in order to discover for themselves.

In addition to the math concept time of the day, we reinforce math skills in any appropriate area of the curriculum. Math skills can be reinforced with literature books, in social studies with graphs and charts, and in science with comparisons of sizes, weights, and measurements.

At this point in our working with multi-age, multi-ability groups, we still feel most comfortable having a distinct math concept time in addition to integrating math into the remainder of the curriculum. While we believe that this good foundation is necessary, we also want to include time for students to explore and experiment for themselves.

■ INFUSING HIGHER-LEVEL THINKING SKILLS

We challenge students to use higher-level thinking skills in every aspect of their learning. For example, they are encouraged to think of many solutions, instead of just one, to a problem. Students are asked to explain the reasoning behind their answers. In our thematic study of communities this year, students used application and synthesis to create individual maps with certain land and water forms. They had learned the six geographical terms *island, peninsula, coast, bay, river,* and *lake.*

Another example of how we used higher-level thinking skills was when we compared the communities of Kentucky, the United States, and Japan. That was an interesting task that forced students to stretch their definition of community. The students had expressed interest in the flags of each of these communities, so we developed a lesson that focused on flags. The students had studied what the symbols on each flag represent and speculated about why the flags might have such symbols. Our follow-up to this lesson involved the creativity skills of originality, flexibility, and elaboration. We challenged the students to use their understanding of symbols to create a flag to represent their primary team community. In order to do this, they had to define what their team meant and stood for. We asked the students to try to think of symbols that stood for their ideas about the team. They also wrote a brief description of their flag, why they chose the colors they did, and what the symbols represented.

During a thematic unit on Change, our learning focused on different forms of matter and how they change. Students were presented with different forms of matter, such as a jar of water, a jar of ice, a carrot, and a nail placed in water. Then they formed hypotheses about if and how each item might change and made predictions as to how long it might take for that change to occur. Over the course of two weeks, the general education students charted the rates and types of change. They analyzed each reaction to explain the reasons for the change or lack of change. The special needs students created observation logs in which they illustrated how the objects changed over time. Megan, John, and Bobby were able to write brief descriptions of their pictures.

∎ SUMMARY AND HOPES FOR THE FUTURE

In conclusion, it is our hope that the readers of this chapter will realize that our primary program, one of inclusion of special needs students, is not that different from any typical primary program. It doesn't require a great deal of extra work or planning. An effective multi-age, multi-ability primary program inherently contains the elements conducive to teaching any child. The aim of any primary program is to address individual differences, support continuous progress, and provide an environment in which the whole child can learn.

REFERENCES

Ahlberg, N. (1989). *Ten in a Bed*. NY: Vikings Children's Books.

Barath, Corton (1976). *Mathematics Their Way*. Menlo Park, CA: Addison-Wesley.

Burke D., Snider, A., and Symonds, P. (1980). *Box It or Bag It Mathematics*. Salem, OR: Math Learning Center.

Hutchins, P. (1968). *Rosie's Walk*. NY: MacMillian.

Hutchins, P. (1986). *The Doorbell Rang*. New York: Greenwillow Books, William Morrow and Company, Inc.

Scieszka, J. (1990). *The True Story of the Three Little Pigs*. NY: Vikings Children's Books.

Success in Understanding Mathematics (1972). River Forest, IL: Laidlaw.

Suess. Dr. (1957). *The Cat in the Hat*. NY: Random House.

LEARNING TO ASSESS: TEACHERS, STUDENTS, AND PARENTS TOGETHER

BY KATHY BIRDWHISTELL, SHERI CANN,
WENDY COMBS, AND SUSAN RICHEY
Saffell Street School
Anderson County

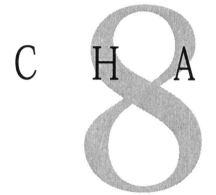

C H A P T E R

Parents observe their children as they grow. Parents record milestones of growth using baby books, height and weight charts, pictures, videos, diaries. They encourage their children and support them along their journey. They watch for signs of sitting up, crawling, and pulling up as stages of learning to walk. They also view babbling as a sign that their children will learn to become social.

Like parents, teachers are also observers of children's growth. But our role as recorders of that growth has changed dramatically over the past few years. Whereas a few years ago our focus was on evaluating products and assigning grades, in today's KERA primary schools, the emphasis is upon documenting the learning process—much as many parents do.

ANECDOTAL REPORTING

Did you record your child's first word, first smile, first step? Parents know what signs to watch for as their children grow. As teachers, we too have become observers looking for steps of progression to record.

Yet, as we begin to alter our role from teacher as examiner to teacher as observer, we found that we not only lacked methods of observing, recording, and analyzing date but aslo confidence in our abilities to make learning observations. But once we got past the stage of doing what we thought others viewed as important, we began to trust ourselves and our expertise. As our confidence grew, so did our choice and use of methods to observe, document, and analyze learning information. More importantly, we began to value how this new role utilized assessment to enrich our teaching and ultimately enrich children's learning, because we had evidence of what children knew and what they appeared to need to learn next. Below we share several of the methods we have used over time as well as examples and comments.

There are many methods or management systems for organizing observations. We have tried using Post-it notes on a grid, cards on a ring, and file folder labels, but we presently use index cards on a clipboard (Capplemann, 1992).

FIGURE 8.1

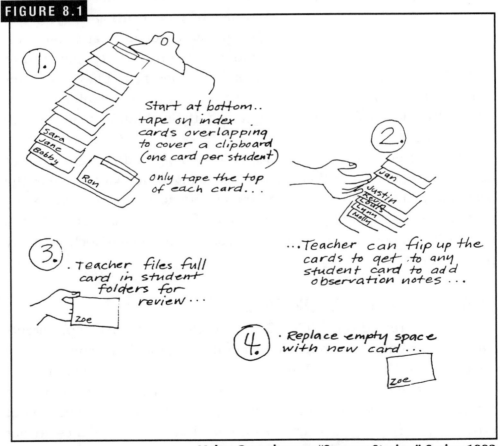

Helen Cappelmann, "Success Stories," Spring 1992

Our clipboards are used to record children's experiences throughout the day. Below are examples of comments on our clipboard:

- Meredyth used the job chart to spell someone's name for a survey (using available print).
- Paul memory-read *I Like* after hearing it once (stage/strategy for reading).
- Clay used a calendar to make a chain on his own to represent the number of days left in school (integration of knowledge).
- Nicholas made a get-well card for Jameson during work time (social development).

Our comments are specific and brief—just enough to be meaningful. We also record just *what* we observe and refrain from evaluating comments (e.g., beautiful get-well cards). The comments are used to chart and document examples of learning experiences. There is no set number of comments, and no right or wrong comment to make. We have found that the more we write, the more we learn about our children and about ourselves as teachers.

■ COLLECTING WORK SAMPLES

One way we track children's growth is to collect work samples to document growth over time. This is dramatically demonstrated in writing samples by Claire (see figures 8.2 a, b, c).

Children's writing can show the natural development of written language. As evaluators in the classroom, we can look at these examples and see how the child has progressed as a writer and to what degree she has use and control of language. Claire progressed from using limited sound associations to using more sounds and some standard words to relate a complete message and finally to creating a story with much detail and thought. Through collecting work samples we were able to track and document Claire's development as a writer.

■ CONFERENCES

What can you learn about a child from talking with him or her? Our classroom instruction is focused around conversations with our

FIGURE 8.2a

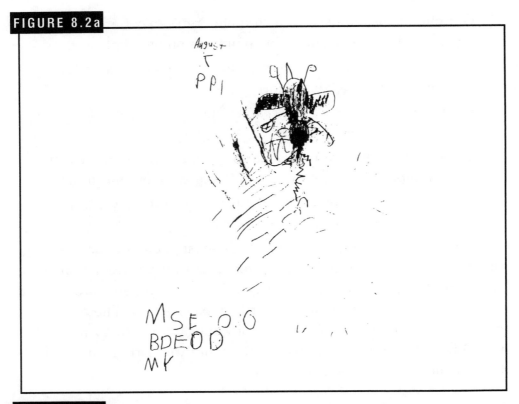

FIGURE 8.2b

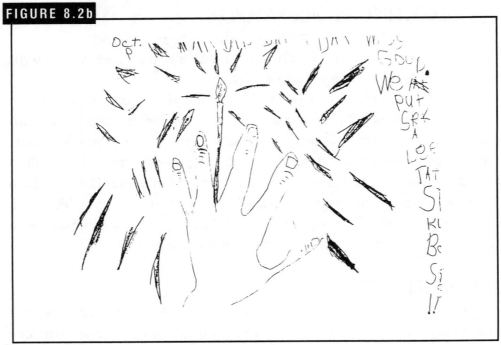

FIGURE 8.2c

Mor. toth coam out of
My' Moth thup! I pit it up
I had lost it at My Gaumae
House the toth hopt up and foun
A pesof cottin And a sow the
cottin as bin lost from
A tent the sow as bin lost
from A baby dall shathin Ifopn
out + at I lost My toth
I look+ But I codit fidit
My moan mall fod it
And she pot it under Her
pilow But the toth fare dinint
come she was goihp to maili+
to me But the toth fare
dit come ~~~~~ I sed it sid
No ho moth sep on me
pleys. I'm as good as you
Oh pleys dr sep on me
pleys rer pop she se p+ on him
soon she fod out that
she had him the tooth
ran unie the ci were
oather th w chet
that had bin ser w it
the le the ci were
thes

without Hertine the thaif
Afder He satine up He wit
out soon the U tooth e viperatid
And teer whs wutine lert
of the little tooth fit A little
bit of sem But oafter Ani+ tooth
groa inti pas And the sow
and cottin eat and bert

f has for All I'm eat
tha permit th=s (Dot come out)

99

children. The information gained is useful in determining individual development and understanding. We conference for a variety of purposes and in a variety of ways. But the importance of a conference is the interaction between the individuals involved.

We developed a Reading Conference Form to keep the conversations focused (see figure 8.3). The form is a conference guide, not a test or a form to be completed for each child. The focus is on the conversation with the child. Conferences are often directed by the child, and this helps us determine how to guide the learner.

Teacher/student conference. Casey was a first-year primary student who came to her teacher to share a book. This began the teacher-student conference with Casey.

Casey: Can I read this to you?

Teacher: Sure, why don't you sit with me?

Casey: (Casey memory-reads Rosie's Walk.)

Teacher: How did you learn to read this book?

Casey: Chris taught me. He read it over and over and then we took turns reading pages and then I just knew how to read it.

Teacher: I'm glad you and Chris are learning to read together.

Casey: Miss Cann, can we read together again tomorrow?

Casey's teacher then recorded the relevant information gained about Casey and her development. First she recorded that Casey was showing interest in reading. She also recorded that Casey could memory-read. Conferences can be recorded on a form, Post-it notes, index cards, an audiotape, or a blank sheet of paper. What is reported is much more important than the method used to record.

Some conferences occur spontaneously. This is not to suggest that as teachers we cannot initiate or plan a conference. Our conferences can be very brief or very detailed, depending on the needs. While we initially focused our conferences in reading and writing, we now conference for a variety of reasons, even simply to get to know the children better.

FIGURE 8.3

Reading Conference Form

Name_____   Date _____

Name of Books

Attitudes & Interests

Print Strategies (phonics, picture clues, sight words, context, etc.)

__ Listening to stories
__ Picture reading
__ Pretend reading
__ Memory reading
__ Recognized some words
__ Recognizes patterns
__ Reading with understanding

Comprehension Strategies

__ Prediction
__ Picture clues
__ Context clues
__ Memory reading
__ Background knowledge
__ Drawing conclusions
__ Justifying opinion

Goals

Peer conferencing. Peer conferencing, students helping students, is another kind of conference we use in our classrooms. The important thing to remember with peer conferencing is that we need to model for students how to communicate and help others. We gradually turn ownership of peer conferencing over to the students. We find that writing "fix-it" groups are a good way to initiate conferences with students.

In "fix-it" groups, students take a piece of their writing and, with help from their peers, talk positively about their good points and about possible ways to improve their texts. This allows children to focus on the content of the piece and provides them a chance to reflect upon themselves as writers. One of the goals of KERA assessments is to help children learn to accurately assess their own work. "Fix-it" groups are one way to do this.

Student-led parent conferences. Student-led conferencing with parents is an effective way for parents to gain knowledge about their children. The teacher becomes an observer and gives ownership of growth to the children. The children's relationships with their parents grow. The connection between the teacher, the students, and their parents becomes another support in the students' educational development. The children run the conferencing by showing their parents samples of work, talking about themselves as learners, sharing accomplishments and interests, and demonstrating their confidence as learners.

Self-evaluation. How do parents know if they have made the right choices for their children? Parents often ask themselves if what they are doing is best for their child. As teachers we have seen and done things that have caused us to evaluate what we are doing in our classrooms. We are teachers who are continually seeking approaches that benefit our classroom instruction. We believe that happens when teachers become self-reflective decision makers in their own classrooms.

Learning to become decision makers in our classrooms has made us aware of the power of self-evaluation. Students need ownership and understanding of their own learning as well. In order to do this, children have to be able to recognize their growth and communicate it to others, setting goals for their future learning. We initiate many different ways for children to evaluate themselves as learners. Among the ways we did this in our classroom were to identify reading goals and to discuss best work.

When our children set reading goals for themselves to become better readers, it helps them take ownership of their reading development. During conferences students are asked to set a goal. This allows them to reflect on themselves as readers and puts some of the responsibility on the student. For example, Christopher decided that he needed to look at pictures to be a better reader. Tate's goal was to read an entire book by herself. Kris said he was going to go to the public library and get books to read to become a better reader. Caleb's goal was to read a chapter book. Our experience is that when students set their own reading goals, it encourages them to take responsibility for their learning and to set a direction for themselves.

"Best work." Choosing best work to be a part of a child's portfolio also helps children self-reflect. When our students look over several pieces of writing and choose what is important and what they value as good writing, we as teachers gain insight into students' abilities to understand and communicate what is valued in writing. For example, in one of our classrooms, Brian said, "I worked real hard and people learned from my story." Brian knows that stories teach us things. He also knows the value of working hard. Jimmy commented, "I like it and it makes me feel like I'm on the beach." Jimmy takes writing personally and knows that it can make him have different emotions. Shea said, "I think it is my best because Mrs. Cann read us a book called *Dinner Time* and this is like it." Shea values what other authors do and sees herself as an author as well.

We do not allow self-evaluation to stop with just reading and writing; we encourage it to be a part of all areas. We believe that teachers need to develop self-assessment approaches that work in their own classrooms and evaluation strategies that examine the learning that is taking place. We began by thinking about what we wanted to accomplish and designed what fit the needs in our classrooms. Our constant question was, "Did it accomplish its purpose?" Two examples of self-evaluation tools that have worked in our classrooms are the Lily Pad Report (see figure 8.4) and the Project Report (see figure 8.5).

FIGURE 8.4

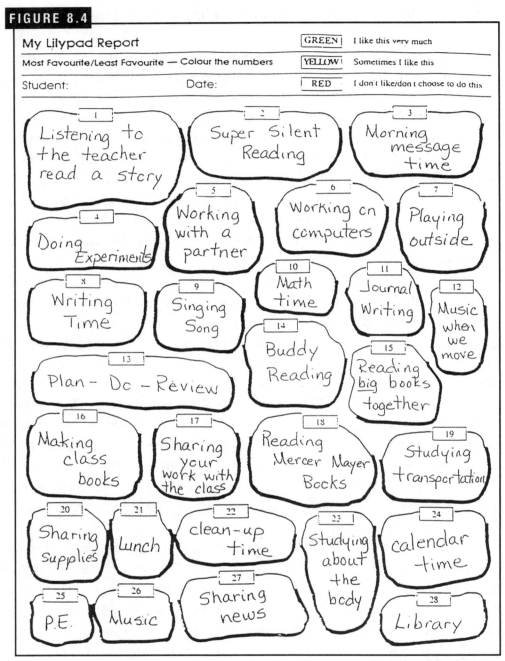

My Lilypad Report

Most Favourite/Least Favourite — Colour the numbers

Student: Date:

GREEN	I like this very much
YELLOW	Sometimes I like this
RED	I don't like/don't choose to do this

1. Listening to the teacher read a story
2. Super Silent Reading
3. Morning message time
4. Doing Experiments
5. Working with a partner
6. Working on computers
7. Playing outside
8. Writing Time
9. Singing Song
10. Math time
11. Journal Writing
12. Music when we move
13. Plan – Do – Review
14. Buddy Reading
15. Reading big books together
16. Making class books
17. Sharing your work with the class
18. Reading Mercer Mayer Books
19. Studying transportation
20. Sharing Supplies
21. Lunch
22. clean-up time
23. Studying about the body
24. calendar time
25. P.E.
26. Music
27. Sharing news
28. Library

**Linda Picciotto, "Collecting Data for Evalution,"
South Park School, Victoria, B.C.**

FIGURE 8.5

Name _Claire_ {My Project} Date _March 1993_

The purpose of my project was _tell others_
about marie curie's life

I worked ☐ alone ☑ with others

This is what I did: Decoriated a box
read   a   book   on   marie curie
gather   things   that helep
tell   her   life story   present the
story,

I shared my project _in font of the_
class   and sharded part of the Project and
then   shea sharded some and   tammy sheardsome

The most important part was _makeing sure_
every one   new evry thing they can
about   marie curie

I think this project _not only tot_
the   class about maria curie but it
also   tot me   about her Justby
Doing   it!

The key for us is to learn from our children and let them help guide the instruction in the classroom.

■ PROGRESS REPORTS

How can a letter grade communicate to parents what their children are doing in the classroom? Because we changed the ways we assess in the classroom we also needed to change the way we reported progress. We developed our own progress reports that fit our instruction. We began by developing student goals to keep us focused in the classroom. We tried reporting on those goals to evaluate their effectiveness but knew we needed more to facilitate good communication. So we viewed other types of reporting and decided what would be most useful for reporting our classroom instruction. Our classrooms typically include large blocks of work time for students. Schedules should be flexible according to the needs of the students and should change as the children develop.

After considering our instructional day and our student goals, we developed our progress report (see figure 8.6).

This report includes bench marks that match our instructional design, large blocks of space for narrative reporting, and a place for parents to set home goals.

One of our fears was that this progress report would eventually become set in stone like the traditional report card had been. We know that evaluation needs to be ongoing and constantly updated and changed. We expect we will change our reporting methods as needed.

■ PORTFOLIOS

What do parents keep to remember their children's growth? We asked ourselves that same question as teachers. Teachers in Kentucky are now using portfolios as a way to show growth in the classroom. Portfolios include concrete examples of what a child can do, and they show parents what children are doing in the classroom. The following is a list of items we include in our portfolios:

FIGURE 8.6

Saffell Street School
Primary Progress Report

Student _____   Teacher _____

LANGUAGE AND LITERACY

DISPLAYS INTEREST IN PRINT

_____ shares books with others
_____ chooses to spend time with books
_____ asks to be read to
_____ listens attentively to books in a group
_____ contributes to group discussions
_____ checks out books frequently

DURING SUPER SILENT READING

| Involves self intensely with print | Maintains interest in print with additional support | Has difficulty being involved with print |

DURING GROUP READING

| Totally involved with reading experiences | Willing to participate with additional support | Unable to stay involved with group activity |

DURING READING DISCUSSIONS

| Carries on a meaningful conversation about reading | Willing to answer questions about reading material with guidance | Unable to express thoughts or feelings about reading materials |

DISPLAYS INTEREST IN WRITING

_____ chooses to write or draw
_____ wanting more writing time
_____ wants to share their writing
_____ shows interest in others writing
_____ uses available print

DURING WRITING WORKSHOP

| Shows independence using the writing process | Shows some independence needing individual guidance to progress | Needs individual guidance to participate |

STORY DEVELOPMENT

| Develops and organizes ideas with a purpose | Expresses logical and sequential thoughts and ideas; needs to develop a clearer purpose | Expresses ideas; may or may not be logically connected |

KNOWLEDGE OF MECHANICS

| Able to use punctuation, capitals, grammer and complete sentences | Shows some use of punctuation, capitals, grammer and complete sentences but not completely | Needs awareness punctuation, capitals, grammer and complete sentences |

READING STRATEGIES (e.g. picture clues, context, background knowledge, phonics)

| Uses a variety of reading strategies | Beginning to use one or more reading strategies | Unaware of reading stratigies |

STEPS IN READING

_____ listening to stories, unaware of print and its functions
_____ picture reading, describing pictures
_____ pretends reading, turning pages, tracking print, rehearsing silently
_____ memory reading
_____ recognizes some words but not all
_____ recognizes patterns in reading
_____ reading with understanding, summarizes

FIGURE 8.6–CONTINUED

Student _____   Date _____

MATH

PROBLEM SOLVING

| Able to problem solve independently | Can use problem solving with some guidance | Needs assistance to solve problems |

COMMUNICATE MEANING

| Using symbols and words to show meaning | Using symbols and/or words needing assistance to show meaning | Needs assistance to use symbols and/or words to show meaning |

NUMBER UNDERSTANDING

| Demonstrates and extends understanding about number meaning | Demonstrates understanding about number meaning | Beginning to show awareness of number meaning |

LISTENING AND SPEAKING

FOLLOWS DIRECTIONS

| Almost always follows directions independently | Working to develop better listening skills to follow through with directions | Needs constant assistance in following directions |

COMMUNICATES IDEAS VERBALLY

| Willing and able to communicate effectively with others | Willing to express thoughts; working to develop a clearer focus | Needs encouragement to express ideas |

PERSONAL AND SOCIAL GROWTH

USE OF TIME

| Is productive and involved | Sometimes needs encouragement to use time productively | Needs assistance to become involved in productive activities |

EFFECTIVE GROUP MEMBER

| Works well with others | Needs limited assistance to work with others | Has difficulty working with others |

COOPERATES WITH PEERS AND SCHOOL PERSONNEL

| Shows respect and gets along well with others | Needs encouragement with limited guidance | Needs constant reminding of how to cooperate |

PARENTS! Please write a home goal for your child. It may be something that you will continue to work on during this next reporting period.

_____   _____
Sign and return   Date

- student work samples that show the student's abilities
- writing samples from the beginning of the year to the end (student chosen and teacher chosen)
- conference sheets
- anecdotal observations
- assessment tools such as Clay's (1982) Running Records
- audiocassette of a child reading
- parent questionnaires
- copies of progress reports
- student self-evaluation forms
- reading log entries
- student-chosen "best work" of any kind

While each portfolio has the same components, each one looks different because of the student's uniqueness. Some will have more of one item than another, according to the learner's individual needs and our instructional purposes. Some students may have more conference sheets because of our need to guide and assess them more often. The beauty of the portfolio is that it is a collection of work samples, student thoughts, assessment tools (both teacher and student), "best work," and any other items that show the student as an individual. Our portfolios are not a final product but an ongoing collection of work that shows growth in learning. Although these are the current components of our portfolios we recognize that, as we do with instruction and progress reporting, we need to revise them according to our students' needs.

■ CONCLUSION

Some teachers might say, "Well, that's okay for you, but I'm not allowed to do that," or, "My students and parents are different from yours." That's the whole point. We are all individuals and unique to our situations. Teachers need to seek out and involve themselves in alternative methods of instruction and evaluation that best fit their students' needs as well as their own. We have learned not to be afraid to step out and try a new idea, whether someone else's or our own. We have also learned not to be satisfied with what someone else says is good to do. We evaluate what is best for our students and ourselves, and we never quit seeking. To say that we are finished or that we have the final product would be to say that our journey has ended. Our journey will continue as long as we seek to improve our own thoughts and ideas for our future classrooms.

REFERENCES

Capplemann, H. (1992). *Success Stories Newsletter*. Santa Monica, CA: Goodyear.

Clay, M. M. (1982). *Observing young readers*. Exeter, NH: Heinemann.

Hutchins, P. (1968). *Rosie's Walk*. NY: MacMillian.

CHALLENGES OF MAKING TRANSITIONS

> We are not content to rest on the accomplishments we have made thus far, but instead we are looking at ways in which our educational journey can continue. . . . That is not to say that our journey has been easy; it is indeed tiresome at times. Yet, every time we begin to get bogged down or frustrated . . . , we are reminded of what has happened in Kentucky. . . . We have traveled many miles, but we know the challenge continues to be ahead of us.
>
> Bridget Baker and Lisa Smith
> Ward Chapel Elementary School

As captured in this quote, teachers undertaking reform initiatives such as the primary program find themselves challenged by the many changes they confront. Yet, in reflecting on their journeys, they take pride in their accomplishments and feel empowered by their shared efforts and determination to continue. Each of the next three chapters offers a portrait of teachers facing—and meeting—challenges in making transitions.

FACING THE SEVEN
CRITICAL ATTRIBUTES

BY BRIDGET BAKER
AND LISA SMITH
Ward Chapel Elementary
Bell County Schools

CHAPTER 9

■ WARD CHAPEL ELEMENTARY: BACKGROUND

The single-story building sits directly along rural US 25E in the southeastern corner of Kentucky. In 1953, eight one- and two-room schoolhouses were consolidated to create Ward Chapel Elementary, the first such school in the Bell County School System. In its forty-year existence, the building has moved from being the newest to being the oldest. From the outside, nothing would indicate that anything out of the ordinary, much less exceptional, could be happening inside. It does not appear to merit its selection, in 1992, as one of twelve National Alliance for Restructuring Education sites.

So, how did 275 preschool through sixth grade students, 82 percent of whom are classified as economically deprived, become participants in the National Alliance? How did Ward Chapel become a "Break the Mold School" in the New American Schools Development Corporation? We believe that it all began with Ward Chapel's primary program and some hardworking and dedicated teachers.

It is often dark in the mountains at 6:55 A.M. as the first bus arrives at Ward Chapel. Two teachers are on early bus duty as the children unload and head to their classrooms. At 7:30 A.M. the ten members of the primary team are in the library meeting for their common planning time. The teachers work together until 8:00 on the agenda for the week, which is prepared by one of the teachers, a responsibility they rotate weekly. The agenda includes discussion of unit activities, special needs students, reports, deadlines, and upcoming meetings. Sometimes more pressing items come up, such as "What's for lunch?" and the teachers get off the published agenda, but for the most part it helps keep the group on task. Throughout the school day the teachers often meet in pairs as they team teach or work together in the afternoons after the children have gone home. Because our school is located directly along the highway, people often make comments about seeing our vehicles in the parking lot late in the evenings. But Ward Chapel's reputation for having teachers who put in long hours began even before the passage of KERA and our selection as a National Alliance school.

In the spring of 1991 the Kentucky Department of Education announced plans to create fourteen primary program pilot sites across the state, and grant funds were made available. Applicants were encouraged to be innovative in developing proposals, which could serve as models for implementing primary program strategies. In their pilot year, these sites would serve as resource schools for others as they prepared for statewide implementation of the primary program. We decided to write a proposal, and in doing so, we addressed all seven of Kentucky's critical attributes, even though full implementation of primary was not mandated statewide for several more years. We were thrilled to be designated a pilot site.

The state department had distributed to all elementary schools a list of critical attributes in a successful primary program. This list also contained examples of various strategies and techniques that could be used to achieve the different critical attributes. Through heated discussions it became apparent that our staff's biggest concern was with developmentally appropriate practices and multi-age/multi-ability classrooms. We talked repeatedly about the different ways we had learned to read, and phonics vs. whole language debates became a regular part of our meetings. Because most had never been involved in a true whole language classroom (except the language experience strategies of the past), we were not convinced that "whole language" could be used successfully with children. Members of the group also expressed concern about the multi-age groupings of children in one classroom. The phrase "like having three split grades" was often heard. Split-grade classes were not well liked by teachers. Regardless of our differing opinions, developmentally appropriate practice and multi-age groupings were key elements the state mandated for the primary program. Personal misgivings aside, these techniques would be the ones we would be implementing.

To make the kinds of changes we knew we had to make, our team decided to first face the issues of overall change. We acknowledged up front that we would experience stress and a variety of other emotions as we adapted our teaching styles and strategies to be more aligned with the spirit of KERA. We decided not to chastise ourselves if we tried something that did not work. That would be part of the change process. Little did we know how many times this thought would be put to the test throughout the year.

One of the hardest lessons for us to learn was that we could disagree about an issue as professionals (and disagree we did!) and not take the disagreement personally and let it affect our friendships. Furthermore, we had to admit to ourselves that not everyone could, or ever would, buy into the notion of developmentally appropriate classrooms. It was frustrating, but by the summer's end we had made great progress indeed.

In August our work became more intense and somewhat frenzied. We knew that we would be held accountable for implementing our program according to our grant, and the task ahead was enormous. On paper we had created "our ideal" primary program, but by September we would face the monumental task of implementing this program. The challenge ahead was significant. We knew that we still had some misgivings as individuals, and yet at the same time, others throughout the state would be coming to observe us in their attempts to prepare to implement their own primary programs. We felt a responsibility to make sure the program we modeled was true to the spirit of the program and to KERA.

■ APPROACHING THE CRITICAL ATTRIBUTES

To help the reader understand Ward Chapel's design for our primary program, it would be useful to look at Kentucky's critical attributes and those particular "bullets" we chose to implement at our school. As we repeatedly stressed to all our visitors, we are working with Kentucky's guidelines to create the primary program that works for us and meets the needs of our students. There is no one right way or exact formula for primary. Below we share the important steps we took to achieve each primary attribute. We will discuss how we initially addressed each attribute and then how we have adapted and changed in our second and third years of implementation.

Critical Attribute #1: Developmentally Appropriate Practice

■ integrate curriculum through thematic studies

■ order manipulatives and begin widespread use

■ establish child-initiated learning—student selection of studies, projects, and independent learning activities

■ initiate whole language approach

■ initiate cooperative learning and use of learning centers

Integrated curriculum. The Ward Chapel primary teachers began their quest for an integrated curriculum by pooling all their teaching supplies and resources together from all subject areas at the direct request of the principal. Mr. Elliott told the teachers, "If you have materials that were purchased by Ward Chapel or the district, then they are to be put in the teacher resource room and shared by all." The school's site-based council allocated one section of an old classroom as a teacher resource/planning room. It is from this room that teachers could check out and store materials for classroom units.

Because classroom materials are always limited, the notion of sharing teacher supplies is logical. However, this has been very difficult. Teachers are often slow to learn the lesson they teach their students about having a pool of shared materials and resources. Some materials are misplaced (forever), and establishing an adequate record-keeping system for sharing was a nightmare. As educators we are so accustomed to purchasing materials with our own money, keeping our own separate files, keeping different program materials separate (e.g., Chapter One, kindergarten, and special education) that it was a challenge to learn to share freely with everyone in the building. Our teachers shared *ideas* readily and freely but the "hands-on" sharing of *materials* proved to be far more difficult. It continues to be an issue we struggle with, and teachers can still be heard crying out, "Whoever's got [some book], please return it to the resource room!"

Ward Chapel's primary teachers wanted to integrate the curriculum through a thematic approach. Prior to our selection as a primary pilot site, we had even polled our students each spring for topics that they would like to study. From these suggestions we developed our thematic studies. We thought that teaching thematically would be one of the easiest tasks to undertake and that it would be nonthreatening to most of the staff.

The primary teachers created their first two thematic units in their summer Monday meetings. As a team of teachers we used all of our resources and expertise to help one another create the units. Published materials also helped us get started. In retrospect, though, we would warn others not to rely too heavily on published materials. Many current thematic units are worksheet-oriented and work against a child-centered environment. In our group meetings we also discussed our classroom centers and what should be included in each unit. We also created a whole language resource list for each unit to help the teachers make the thematic studies expand throughout the school day.

Our very first unit was "All About Me." It was a totally integrated unit that went completely across the curriculum. For the first three weeks of school we celebrated the individuality and uniqueness of each child through classroom activities.

At the end of the "All About Me" integrated unit, we were definitely feeling pressure from some of the parents. They were saying things like, "My kids are having fun, but when will they be bringing the math book home?" or, "What social studies book is my child using?" But our first unit was anything but a textbook approach. Our walls were lined with student charts, graphs, and reports. The classrooms were places of active learning where students were examining, writing, estimating, and demonstrating. Everything we were doing was hands-on, and the children were exploring and learning in centers. In each classroom students continuously built positive self-concepts with activities that focused on each student as an individual and how it is OK to be different.

We sat down together and looked at exactly what we were doing in our classrooms during this time. We were amazed at all of the "skills" we had covered. But even with all of these wonderful child-centered activities, we had doubts about what our unit had accomplished when the parents questioned us. There was no doubt that they were having fun because the students were often heard saying, "We played" whenever they were asked what they had done at school. Many parents (and teachers) do not associate play with learning. In our initial contacts with parents about primary school, we failed to communicate that when children are learning in a nonthreatening environment and are meeting with success, school is indeed fun. Although the parents did not have worksheets to document their children's progress, a great deal of learning was definitely taking place. But while we assured the parents that this was true, we were still learning the lesson for ourselves.

The "All About Me" unit was followed by a six-week content theme unit, "The Weather." For this unit we relied heavily on a textbook/worksheet-oriented approach. (Are we slow learners, or what?) This approach was not as successful as we had imagined because it was not child-centered, and it created problems with our classroom groupings. Our afternoon thematic classes consisted of six- through nine-year-olds. There was such a wide span of abilities in each class that not everyone in a group was capable of doing the same activity to the same criteria. We had to move students toward high expectations but still allow for students' differences. In our common planning time we discussed this dilemma. One early suggestion was to have "high" and "low" worksheets for each thematic unit, but this approach set limitations on what the children could achieve. We found that thematic units of study had to be more flexible. We continued to explore and *change* (there's that word again) the way we attempted our thematic units. After reading and observing others, we tried an all-learning-centers approach to a unit on Kentucky. This unit allowed for more student individuality and cooperative learning activities. This change better met the needs of our multi-ability classrooms.

In the past year, unit development has shifted from our original concerns to a focus on Kentucky's six Learning Goals and seventy-five Learner Outcomes, which are the basis of Kentucky's curriculum framework. (These outcomes are also the measure for student performance on our statewide assessment.) We now all work together as a team to create every unit of study, as opposed to working individually or in pairs. Each unit is completely activity centered. The activities are different from unit activities of the past in that now all activities are aligned directly with a student outcome. In previous units we were guilty of creating wonderful, exciting activities without being sure of their purpose. Now we are aware of what outcome we are working toward, and a performance event for monitoring student progress flows directly from these activities. We realize that a good unit is more than good activities. Our challenge is to create units that help students make the connections between all learning and apply those skills in real-world situations.

Understanding and implementing whole language. As a group, we knew that using a whole language approach fit with developmentally appropriate practice encouraged by the state. However, not all team members were comfortable abandoning their former beliefs about the way children learn to read. Our teachers talked extensively and passionately of their beliefs about the ways children learn to read and write. Overall, we had a very limited comfort zone when it came to the direct implementation of a total whole language philosophy.

To get our schoolwide philosophy off the ground, we came up with a list of whole language strategies that each teacher would feel comfortable and confident applying in his or her classroom. In the first year we agreed that we would each do the following: read aloud to our classes everyday; establish paperback libraries in each classroom; have a scheduled silent reading time each day (even if the students appeared to be wasting time and not "reading"); have each student maintain a writing journal (that we wouldn't correct for grammar); create and maintain whole language portfolios for each student; have student-maintained reading logs; and allow students to begin reading and writing at whatever level they were currently functioning (regardless of their age). However, the teachers' consensus was to continue to rely on the basals as their students' instructional text during that first year.

With the school year in full swing, Bridget felt frustrated when she noticed her primary children complaining about the basal books being ones they had already read. Her reading group consisted of a majority of students who had already been through the basals at that level. Being frustrated by the students' inability to work productively with the all-too-familiar texts, she abandoned the basals and put them in the reading corner. She used nursery rhymes and fairy tales and other great works of literature to teach reading the remainder of the school year. During the school year her students made gains and progressed as much as their counterparts in the other classrooms who were still relying on the basal programs.

Meanwhile, midway through the first year, the remainder of the primary teachers were beginning to feel frustrated by the limitations of the basal program and decided that they would each create five literature-based units to use on an alternating basis as a replacement for the basal readers. The team of primary teachers left school one Friday full of enthusiasm regarding the literature units they were going to develop and begin using in place of their basal program. As the teachers arrived at school Monday morning, however, the stress of creating literature units was most visible. Teacher comments included, "Do you know how long I worked on this?" and, "There's no way I'm going to be able to do this." Developing literature-based units without direct support proved to be a very difficult task. Thus, change was somewhat slow and painful the first year.

As the teachers experimented with various whole language strategies, we still worried that our students would not grasp the necessary skills in reading and writing. By year's end, however, teachers who were skeptical about the whole language philosophy found that the strategies used resulted in learners who were becoming self-motivated readers and writers. Mrs. Bisceglia, one of our veteran teachers, talked excitedly about how effectively our students were handling comprehension questions, how their listening skills had developed, and how they were becoming more expressive in their oral and written language skills. An even greater testimony to our teachers' belief in whole language was that the primary teams unanimously decided to use only trade books for reading instruction the following school year. The school's intermediate team joined the primary team in using literature as the major focus in their language arts program as well. That was a long way from our original list of minimum compliance! The teachers' commitment is real and genuine, and the children are excited about reading. There's no doubt that when children can read the books they enjoy, reading becomes a purposeful activity they love to take part in.

Critical Attribute #2: Multi-Age/Multi-Ability Classrooms

■ establish heterogeneous family groupings by age and ability

Family groupings. Ward Chapel originally began its primary experience by creating family homebases with approximately twenty multiage/multi-ability (MAMA) students aged five through nine in each self-contained class. Our homebase groupings were created randomly, with some minor adjustments to allow for equal distribution of boys, girls, and special needs students. Each homebase classroom was intended to be a representative sample of the school's actual student population.

At Ward Chapel, a student's assignment to a family homebase grouping is stable, and a child remains with the same class and teacher throughout the primary experience. Changes in a homebase assignment happen naturally as children exit the primary program at fourth grade and new students enter at the kindergarten level.

One of the strongest benefits of the MAMA grouping is the development of a family atmosphere. Students spend time with both younger and older children, and relationships develop that are much like sibling relationships. Because these family groupings remain together throughout the primary experience, the children and the teacher get to know one another, providing continuity in the educational program. Teachers learn about the social, emotional, physical, aesthetic, and cognitive capabilities of each student and keep adding to this knowledge base each year.

Critical Attribute #3: Continuous Progress

■ help students progress at own rate as determined by authentic assessment

■ promote social, emotional, physical, aesthetic, cognitive development—the "whole child"

■ establish success-oriented, noncompetitive environment

In the beginning, parents and teachers were uneasy about putting the younger and the older students together. One concern was that the older students would teach the younger ones bad habits. In reality, while some less than desirable behaviors may be learned, many more wonderful ones pass from older to younger students. The biggest concern seems to involve the inclusion of five-year-olds, and this continues to be debated statewide. Ward Chapel began its primary program by including five-year-olds for their total instructional day. Since the state's requirements for inclusion of five-year-olds changed after we had already established a full three-hour day for these students, we hesitated about changing our program just because other schools were experiencing difficulty. At present we are examining our past experiences with including five-year-olds and attempting to determine what degree of involvement is best for our students.

Flexible, heterogeneous groupings. Our first attempts at primary MAMA scheduling included instructional periods for whole language, reading skill groups, thematic studies, and math instruction. The math groupings were created by assessing the students' strengths and skills and then placing them into one of three instructional groups. Initially, the plan was to make the math groups flexible so that students could move into an instructional group as their progress indicated. What actually happened was that each of the groups moved steadily along, but no movement was made between the groups. We had created exactly what we did not want—stagnant skill groups. Learning from this by reflecting on our teaching has helped us change our grouping strategies.

Continuous progress. The primary program at Ward Chapel allows children to progress at their own rate rather than fit into a grade-specific curriculum. For example, one activity in Lisa's multi-age math class had the students all working on linear measurement. The students were instructed to measure any three items in the room. Some of the children chose to measure with nonstandard items such as paper clips and pieces of yarn, while others in the classroom were using rulers, yardsticks, meter sticks, and tape measures. The children recorded their measurements in various ways. Products varied from drawings of measurements, to detailed written descriptions of measuring techniques, to simple listings of objects measured and their sizes. The children were working in this noncompetitive environment without a fear of failure.

Critical Attributes #4 and #5: Authentic Assessment and Qualitative Reporting

- emphasize observing, examining multiple/varied work samples
- document social, emotional, physical, aesthetic, and cognitive development
- be descriptive, using narrative
- reflect a continuum of pupil progress
- use varied formats (portfolios, journals, videotapes, narratives)

Statewide authentic assessment. As educators in Kentucky, we have been fortunate to have a statewide assessment system that focuses on authentic assessment for fourth, eighth, and twelfth grades. This assessment includes performance-event testing and student portfolios in math and writing. Kentucky has also established a curriculum framework that is based on six learning goals and seventy-five learner outcomes. All statewide assessment is a measure of student performance toward these goals and outcomes. Because the state assessment happens at the "end" of primary, there is a need to maintain an authentic assessment focus in the primary years.

The state is also in the draft stages of a Kentucky Early Learning Profile (KELP). The KELP is an instrument aimed at helping teachers document students' growth through anecdotal recordings. This instrument will be used to show progress and will also serve as the tool for reporting to parents. The KELP provides for parent and student interviews and conferences and teachers' observational records. In addition, the KELP contains student performances that span the total curriculum to give an accurate picture of the child's abilities. Two such activities that a child will complete include researching a question and developing a personal timeline.

Ward Chapel has been involved with the KELP since its beginning, when Bridget Baker served as one of fifty pilot teachers. In the second year the KELP pilot expanded to 400 teachers, and the entire Ward Chapel primary team was selected to pilot the KELP as a schoolwide effort. Our selection to participate in KELP was welcomed because we had been looking for a more efficient and organized way to document student progress. Each individual teacher was experimenting with his or her own strategies for maintaining and evaluating student performance according to some general school guidelines. Many of these methods were effective for us as individuals. However, we often met as a group when student information was required for district and state reports. We wanted to make sure that all teachers were recording similar student information and that we were thoroughly representing all children.

Schoolwide authentic assessment. Prior to our selection as a KELP pilot school, Ward Chapel had also begun efforts to establish a school portfolio for each child. This procedure became a key component in our professional development plan to assure that all teachers, not just those for fourth grade, were working toward the learning goals and outcomes. This system requires all teachers to maintain weekly anecdotal records, student writing samples, math tasks, performance events, and even a technology piece for all students. The school's portfolio is intended to reflect everyday classroom activities and to contain products that naturally flow from the classrooms' active learning environments. As mentioned earlier in the discussion of our thematic units, the true challenge was to create classrooms where learning and assessment go hand in hand and have application to the real world.

Reporting student progress. Creating a quality reporting system that reflects this active learning environment and Kentucky's seventy-five learner outcomes continues to be one of our most challenging tasks. In our first two years of primary, Ward Chapel's teachers experimented with nongraded report cards. One format was created by a local district committee. As a first attempt this was a tool that utilized many components that other nongraded schools had used to report to parents. Our staff took this report card and mandated parent conferences, since it was so different from previous report cards. In our first attempt at report card conferences, over 95 percent of our parents attended their scheduled meetings to find out about their child's progress. Initial parent concerns focused mostly on the absence of traditional grades because students received a mark to indicate whether progress was made consistently, frequently, with help, or seldom. One parent even asked which mark should earn her child $1.00 in the traditional report card payoff. The bottom line for parents was whether or not they should be concerned about their child's performance. We spent the conference time showing parents samples of their child's work and how this aligned with the new report card. The narrative format provided parents with additional information about their child's progress.

The positive aspects of experimenting with the report cards led us to decide to use the KELP as the basis for documenting student performance and reporting to parents. The intermediate team will be using the school's portfolio as its key document in reporting student progress. Parent conferences will again be an integral part of sharing information about students' progress toward the six learning goals and outcomes.

Critical Attribute #6: Professional Teamwork

- ■ secure a regular time for planning/sharing
- ■ team teach, collaboratively teach, and peer coach
- ■ promote regular communication among all professional staff (physical education, music, art, special education, gifted, Chapter One, and so on)

Gaining a shared vision. Ward Chapel's diversified faculty has been an asset in the development of our primary program. Our staff's professional experience now ranges from four to twenty-eight years in fields from preschool to kindergarten to technology to special education. The fifteen teachers actively sought sources of training and professional development. Mr. Larry Elliott, the building principal, insisted that every Ward Chapel primary teacher and the school's librarian attend the state's own summer Primary Institute to gain primary program knowledge. He also provided funding for every teacher to attend an additional summer training literacy program.

To further prepare for implementing the primary program, our teachers met every Monday morning throughout the summer prior to our selection as a primary pilot site. We realized that implementing the ideas behind the primary program would take time and teamwork. Little did we know that our nonmandated meetings together were the beginnings of an even stronger partnership.

Common planning time. Ward Chapel began its first attempt at common planning time by using itinerant teachers three days a week. The only way we could arrange for all primary teachers to be free at the same time was to have both the physical education teacher and the music teacher combine two classes of primary students at the same time for one instructional class. Needless to say this was a less than ideal situation. While these four classes were with these two itinerant teachers, another classroom was having art and the sixth class was in the library. This allowed all six primary classroom teachers to meet and plan together for forty-five minutes three days a week.

The principal saw a need for even more planning time, and he *changed* the schedule in the middle of the school year to give the teachers an additional thirty minutes. This was created by having the teachers report to work ten minutes before the actual school day began and then having instructional aides supervise the students while the teachers were in the breakfast room. This early-morning planning proved to be one of the most effective planning periods for our teachers because we begin each day focused on our purpose of working together for students. Our teachers have also agreed to stay after school for thirty minutes twice a week to meet with their school team. The only other planning we have managed to schedule during the school day without additional staff is individualized planning. Teachers might schedule their classes together for a particular lesson to allow for some special activities, thus freeing up teachers for individualized planning. This time for common planning has allowed teachers to share their experiences and build a stronger commitment toward "our" students.

Collaboration. When we established our primary program, our desire was to continue the trend of the school's past experiences toward less "pull-out" to meet student needs. Ward Chapel had already been moving toward a more inclusive model with collaboration and consultation between the special education and regular educators. Special education students go through all of the due process procedures to determine their potential for being educated in the least restrictive environment.

Because 82 percent of Ward Chapel's students are already identified as being at risk and qualify for the Chapter One program, it is easy to see how our special needs students are more similar to than different from our general student population. By combining a schoolwide project approach to Chapter One and a more inclusive model for special learners, Ward Chapel is attempting to create a school environment that meets the specific needs of its students regardless of their classification. Teachers no longer see themselves as serving the students in an isolated role such as by being a Chapter One, a regular classroom, or a special education teacher. There is no longer a "my kids" approach to educating students; teachers are sharing that responsibility. Sharing continues to become easier and more natural as we continue to spend more time planning together.

Critical Attribute #7: Positive Parent Involvement

■ form home/school partnerships

■ form school/community partnerships

■ continuously exchange information

Prior to the implementation of our primary program, parents were introduced to the concepts of "primary" through letters, personal contacts, and Parent-Teacher Organization meetings. All kindergartners and first and second graders took home report cards that said "promoted to *primary program*" with a note explaining this concept again to parents. Teachers also spent time explaining the upcoming changes to their students.

As teachers we worked to create an interest in our pilot primary program. We created a primary program logo. This logo was on every piece of correspondence that went into homes and into the community.

We also created weekly progress reports that all students took home on Friday and that parents signed and returned on Monday. This was an attempt to assure a continuous exchange of information between the school and the home.

Home/community/school partnerships. Our school applied to the state and received a Family Resource Center (FRC) grant through KERA funding. This program, a component of KERA, has been instrumental in helping make the school/home/community connection. Our FRC has worked diligently to strengthen the home/school connection through visits, after-school programs, and information sharing. The FRC has also helped the school build better business/community connections.

The primary staff also solicited parents and the community at large for help in developing our thematic units. Parents and others from the community volunteered and gave school demonstrations for the students. We also developed unit-related home activities that parents and children could complete together. For example, one assignment was for each family to discuss what their children are supposed to do in case of a fire and to have a mock fire drill at their home. These home activities were related directly to our study of "Homes of Long Ago" and were just another way of keeping our parents in touch in a real-life way with our studies in the classroom.

At Ward Chapel we truly believe that the home, school, and community must work closely together to create an effective educational experience. Our faculty is constantly looking for ways to connect these student environments. This is an extremely difficult challenge, given the statistical information about our area. Ward Chapel is located in the Fifth Congressional District, which was identified by the 1990 Census as having the highest percentage of non-high-school graduates of any congressional district in the nation. Sixty-four percent of the adult population in Bell County have not graduated from high school.

Bell County traditionally has relied on coal mining as its chief industry. Coal mining was a high-paying job that did not require a high school diploma. Lured to the mines by these high-paying jobs, many people gave up their pursuit of education. It was not uncommon for college-educated teachers to earn less than the coal miners.

Thus, for decades education was not necessary for employment. But during the past ten years, with the shutdown of many coal mines and with very few other industries in the area, Bell County's unemployment rate has soared. These factors have helped create an under-educated work force that now must hunt for jobs. In addition to the collapse of the coal industry, Bell County must also deal with the cycle of welfare dependency and the 44.6 percent of our county's children who are living in poverty.

As we have implemented our primary program and attempted to improve the statistics of our area, it has become increasingly obvious that our task is monumental and that our school's needs involve more than merely establishing a quality primary program. As teachers we feel the need to gear all of our school programs, from preschool to intermediate to lunchroom to family resource center activities, toward the common goal of helping all our students learn.

■ LOOKING BEYOND OUR PRIMARY PROGRAM

With the selection of Ward Chapel as a state pilot site in the primary program, our doors were opened to visitors from all across the state. Hosting visitors throughout our primary program development has continually forced us to examine our beliefs and our approaches to our program. This process of group and self-analysis has caused us to constantly reevaluate our beliefs as educators. We are striving to implement our school philosophy, which establishes high expectations for all learners.

We are extremely proud of our national recognition, but we are probably even more proud of our accomplishments. Like never before, the entire staff at Ward Chapel has claimed ownership of the children. We are not content to rest on our accomplishments thus far but instead are looking at ways to continue our educational journey. We are constantly reviewing what we have learned and how it can best be adapted to fit the needs of our children, our teachers, and our community. That is not to say that our journey has been easy; it is indeed tiresome at times. Yet every time we begin to get bogged down or frustrated with some bureaucratic pile of paperwork, we are reminded of what has happened in Kentucky. KERA has created a framework for educators to create quality school environments for all learners from primary to high school. As educators at Ward Chapel we have traveled many miles, but we know the challenge continues to be ahead of us.

FROM PHILOSOPHY TO PRACTICE: A CONTINUOUS STRUGGLE FOR EXCELLENCE

BY KAREN ADKINS
Millard Elementary
Pike County

CHAPTER 10

Summer is over and the first students drift into the classroom. Excited voices echo as the students meet classmates from the year before. On their own, some older students show the new primary students the pet rabbits, where their supplies belong, and the materials the room has to offer. Others offer to take the new students to breakfast. They go off hand in hand, talking a mile a minute. Within a few minutes, the room is a buzz of activity. The clock shows 7:30 A.M. School doesn't begin until 8:00, but the students' learning and excitement seem to have no time schedule.

I had tried to envision what the first day of the 1991–92 school year would be like; however, I was still caught off guard. The older students I had had the previous year as kindergarten students, and the new students were those attending school for the first time. We, the staff at Millard Elementary, had read extensively to prepare to pilot the primary program during the 1991-92 school year. Until the students arrived and began telling me about their vacations, though, I hadn't fully realized the benefit of having students more than one year. It hit me at once. I knew these kids! The first day we slipped back into our old relationship, and it felt like being at the controls of a well-oiled piece of machinery. Furthermore, it was as if there were thirteen teachers, instead of just me, to guide the new students. I could feel the sense of pride the older students had in their new-found status. They were now the oldest and wisest, and they eagerly took over the job vacated by the students promoted to upper primary. We were a class, a community, the very first day of school.

▪ MILLARD ELEMENTARY—WHERE IT ALL BEGAN

Our school, located in a mountainous, rural area in far Eastern Kentucky, serves close to 600 students in Head Start, the primary program, and grades four through six. We have a strong parent volunteer group and became a site-based management school in the 1992-93 school year. We have a good reputation, and in April 1993 *Redbook* named us as one of America's best schools.

The first day of school I described occurred as we piloted the primary program in 1991-92. We had volunteered to move ahead of the mandated dates and begin a year earlier than required. Today we are very glad we went ahead. These programs take much energy and hard work and some time for trial and error. KERA is changing the face of education, and we see evidence of that change every day in our classrooms. A new philosophy provides a base for these changes. However, I began the search for this new philosophy years ago, when I was only a student myself.

▪ MY BEGINNINGS

I was an honor student in my high school junior year in Columbus, Ohio, when I eloped and married at the age of sixteen. I had one son when I was barely seventeen, and twenty years later I still am married to the same man. We worked hard throughout the years, but never seemed to get anywhere. All of our struggles taught me many things, gave me a unique outlook on life, and made me a champion for those trying to overcome the odds. I finally found the road to success when I got my GED and decided to go back to school in 1984. I taught Head Start while putting myself through school at Pikeville College. Everything I learned about education I tried in my own classroom. This helped me design my own three-year-old preschool Head Start program.

I student-taught in kindergarten and sixth grade at Pikeville Elementary. The education I received was very good, even though I relied upon the teacher's manual, the textbooks, and the accompanying workbooks. I had only had a traditional education to this point, and I found that something bothered me about what I was doing. I felt restless. I wondered if I would become bored. Where was the excitement? Those restless feelings set me on a quest that is continuing to this very day.

While student teaching, I received a brochure advertising a two-week summer Foxfire Workshop at Berea College. I had learned about Foxfire at an Appalachian Literature Workshop during the summer of 1987. The presenter's English class had been reading *River of Earth*, written by a local author, James Still. The students had written to Still asking questions about his novel, and a project was born between the writer and the class. The presenter glowed as she described the project, her excitement obvious as she outlined the work of her English class. I wasn't going to teach high school English, but I remembered this woman when I looked at the brochure. I knew I was looking for something that was outside the traditional educational realm and decided to apply for the workshop. Little did I know then that attending a workshop for two short weeks would change my thinking forever.

At the workshop we read John Dewey's *Experience and Education*. I learned to think of school as a community of learners working together to make some sense of and be a part of the world. To Dewey, the goal of education was to make students lifelong learners. He felt students' education should be active instead of passive; children should be actively involved with planning, implementing, and evaluating their education. Those of us in the workshop examined how Dewey's philosophy had been the foundation of the Foxfire classes. We read Wiggington's *Sometimes a Shining Moment*, which explains the Foxfire process and the history of its evolution.

I learned a great deal in this workshop, but instead of losing my restless feeling, I found myself wondering what I was going to do with this new learning. That wondering set me on a new road, full of change. I knew in my heart that children learn best by doing, and that inspired me to change from being a traditional teacher to one who would never know all the answers and would continually search for them. I did not really understand the shift I had made until I began to implement changes in my teaching.

■ FOXFIRE JUMP STARTS MY CAREER

Although inundated with textbooks and workbooks at the start of my career, I had become convinced that writing for real purposes was critical. So the English textbook was the first to go, and getting rid of the textbook in one area opened the door to change.

Students begged me to allow them to write a newspaper, so that became our first real project. They learned about the parts of the newspaper and created a bulletin board displaying their new knowledge using newspapers they examined. They felt they needed to see how to put a newspaper together. So they learned to write a business letter and wrote to the local newspaper requesting a tour. The children spent a lot of time learning to brainstorm, to vote, and to accept the majority's idea. The actual writing began, and they conducted interviews, created comics, collected recipes, and wrote movie reviews. A great deal of writing, revision, and editing occurred before the typing and layout began (which the children also did). The newspaper was sold and was a huge success. Foxfire was alive and well in my classroom!

Later that year the students wrote a seven-skit play to teach Halloween safety rules to the rest of the school. Near winter holiday time we began to study Appalachian literature. I had been reading parts of *Kinfolks,* by Gurney Norman, to the students. After the story "The Wounded Man," the students asked their families to tell them one story from their families' pasts, which they wrote down and shared with the class. This assignment snowballed because the students wanted to make the stories into a book. It took until the end of the school year to complete the project. A local printing company produced the book for us, after the children worked to raise the $700 needed.

The Foxfire training combined with my teacher training got my career off to a flying start. I was ready to see how it worked at a new grade level.

■ PREPARING FOR PRIMARY

In the 1990-91 school year, I began teaching kindergarten, and because it was new to me, I met with some old fears. I worried about the emphasis on testing and how to approach reading instruction, but the basals stayed in the cabinet. I found an old chart stand and charts in the basement. I copied nursery rhymes, and we began to read and chant them. My aide put together small journals out of recycled computer paper, and the students and I started writing stories together.

By the end of the year, those who were ready to read were reading. Some were writing simple stories in their journals. Some were still drawing pictures. The children were doing what they could. I also knew that I would have the same children for another year because we were to pilot the primary program.

The more we read and studied about the primary program, the happier I became. Whole language, hands-on math, learning by doing, classrooms run like a democracy, and the teacher as a guide and facilitator formed the core of the KERA philosophy and reflected the kind of teaching I had come to value and demonstrate. The preliminary draft of the Curriculum Framework included the eleven Core Practices of Foxfire in the informational section. I knew those core practices were the backbone of my program and could be matched with KERA's six learning goals. I also discovered that the philosophies of KERA and Foxfire had many elements in common. I felt then as if KERA had become a good friend.

At Millard Elementary, we decided to group children by age: five- and six-year-olds in Lower Primary and seven- and eight-year-olds in Upper Primary, with the understanding that we might have to make some adjustments. We ordered instructional supplies and prepared throughout the summer for the school year. One day the principal said that seventeen of the approximately thirty staff members were at school working on their own time.

That summer I also attended a two-week Level II Foxfire course in which I studied philosophy at greater depth. I found that Dewey was not alone in his beliefs. I read more on whole language and further developed my language arts curriculum. I spent a week learning *Math*

Their Way and put in time at school making materials and finding books in the library to use for children's individual reading. I decorated my room the last day before the school year began.

The year turned out to be very interesting and offered several new changes. I taught a self-contained lower primary class that included some older children with special needs. Later in the year the special education teacher and I began collaborating, which helped greatly. I loved what I was doing and so did the children, but the planning and gathering of materials became enormous tasks. I usually stayed at school two nights a week until 9:00 P.M. I also spent half of either Saturday or Sunday at school. My program was going well, and I was doing many things such as keeping anecdotal records, conducting reading and writing conferences, and keeping progress portfolios. But I felt like a hamster on a wheel! I never caught up, and I felt we missed many instructional opportunities.

Toward the end of that year, we began to plan for the next year. This time KERA mandates helped us plan better. We were expected to write an action plan that addressed many areas we had omitted the first year. And since we were planning our program early, we were able to order materials to support it. It made such a difference to have a year's experience behind us.

As the year drew to a close, I began to evaluate my program. I had done what I had planned to do, but it nearly killed me, and I felt the children were cheated in some ways. Since I could plan and teach only a limited number of lessons, I offered only two levels of material to the children. As in a split-grade classroom, this practice assumed that the children needed either one level or the other. Also, since I almost always worked with one group while the other group worked independently, I found it difficult to observe and guide children's learning. I had flexible groups with children of mixed ages, but I knew I was not providing each student with developmentally appropriate activities.

I felt I needed another person to make it work and found a colleague who felt the same. After I moved into the classroom next to my new team member, we took down a movable wall and made one large room. We were ready for yet another modification in our primary program.

■ TEAMING—A NEW EXPERIENCE

We worked all year in our large one-room environment with forty-seven students. Our classes were based on a whole language philosophy, *Mathematics Their Way*, and all the technology IBM had to offer. Both of our rooms contained five computers and a printer networked with two file servers. We used such IBM instructional programs as Writing to Read, Stories and More, Writing and Publishing Center, TLC Math and Spelling, and Manipulative Math Level I.

The year developed very well, and I felt we met the children's instruction needs better than the previous year. However, I became aware of some drawbacks. The most challenging one for me was developing a sense of community with forty-seven students, a large group. Also, my team teacher had not been trained in Foxfire, which meant we tended to think differently about some things. I found that working as a team meant making adjustments that might not be needed with only one adult in charge.

Also, our schedule changed many times during the beginning of the year. However, after a few months of trial and error, we found a schedule we liked and kept it throughout the rest of the year. Following is a schedule of our daily activities with our students.

8:00–8:15 Handwriting. We taught this in a traditional manner in each homeroom as we took care of paperwork and the children returned from breakfast.

8:15-8:45 DEAR. (Drop Everything and Read) The children chose their own books and read anywhere in the room. Since the older students were familiar with the books, they could read them to the younger children. On Tuesdays and Thursdays, a fifth grade class joined us. Seventy-five students reading out loud sure made a racket, but it was an educational racket!

8:45-9:15 Math Their Way Calendar Activities. All students met in the front of the large room. My team member and I rotated responsibility for teaching this activity each week. During this happy, risk-free time we introduced many concepts from different disciplines. (We used the calendar as the focus, but we introduced the concepts through chants and songs.) The students liked calendar time and participated on a voluntary basis.

9:15-11:10 Language Arts. At this time, we often divided the students into two large groups. My team member often worked with emergent readers, and I worked with children who were at different levels of conventional reading.

My team member began her time with the computer program *Writing to Read.* This is an IBM program that teaches basic phonemes and encourages writing with invented spelling. The children often worked in pairs and rotated through the stations on their own. They took a cookie break at the end of this time. They spent the rest of the time on books that correlated with the theme for the week. The whole group read from big books and then got involved in different levels of literature extension activities.

I began with a reading workshop that had three basic levels. One group chose their own reading material. They kept a log and met with me on Fridays for a conference. The children chose different extension activities to complete, which resulted in a product that was presented to the class and scored with a rubric. A conference followed to help the children evaluate their work. The groups' membership changed often as the children moved toward becoming independent readers. During the last month of school everyone chose their own material and read on an appropriate level.

We conducted a Writers' Workshop during the latter half of the language arts block. We began each day with a minilesson in which I introduced or reviewed specific skills I wanted the students to begin using in their writing. After that they either wrote at the computer or in their journal on a topic of their own choosing, unless we were working on a specific project, such as a class newsletter. The time concluded with children sharing their work. The children wrote a variety of stories, and parent volunteers helped them create books. Each child published a minimum of three books during the year.

11:10-12:00 Theme Time. We alternated between studying a theme with the computer program *Stories and More* and studying a theme of our own choosing. In *Stories and More* the students rotated through the computer station, the activity station, and the listening center. The older students taught the younger ones to use the computer and the mouse. Theme studies we developed on our own were varied. Sometimes we used learning centers and other times the children participated in whole group or partner activities. After theme time the children had a thirty-minute lunch break.

12:40-1:45 Math Their Way, TLC Math, Math Manipulatives Level I. We assessed the students and divided them into two groups. We used stations—teacher, computer, and activities—to correlate the three math programs. New concepts were introduced at the teacher station, old concepts were reinforced at the activity station, and the computer station provided independent practice of new and old concepts and skills. Manipulatives were used every day, and games provided the drill needed for learning some concepts.

1:45-3:00 Center Time. The children returned to their homerooms. Center Time was their favorite part of the day. The students were invited to use any materials in the room. The computers were always in heavy demand. The students always believed that they were playing, but as we looked around, we saw groups reenacting calendar, children typing stories on the computer, or several students sitting in the bathtub reading out loud to one another. This was a time when children returned to an activity they had enjoyed during the day. It was one of those scheduled times when much learning took place without direct teaching.

■ REFLECTIONS

When school ended we knew it had been a productive year. We had many examples of how much the children had learned. Best of all, we liked knowing that each year we would be seeing the same students again. We felt that we would never have to start from scratch again as long as the primary program continued.

Every year since I began teaching, my program has changed. I added what I learned on my own and from others. I continually see new ways to do things, and that makes teaching exciting. My goal is to have the best possible program, so I'm always searching for something to make it better.

KERA has changed education and the teaching profession radically, and teachers are struggling to live up to the standards in the law. I began working on understanding teaching and learning in 1988. For five years I have attended workshops and taken university classes, yet my program still lacks exactly what is spelled out in the law. Although I've made numerous changes, I know there is still room to grow. It is my hope that by recounting my gradual professional development, I have helped others understand that reform can and will work if teachers are given the support and, most important, the time they need to change.

REFERENCES

Baratta-Lorton, M. (1976). *Mathematics their Way*. Menlo Park, CA: Addison-Wesley Publishers.

Dewey, J. (1938). *Experience and Education*. NY: Collier Books.

Norman, G. (1977). *Kinfolks: The Wilgus Stories*. Frankfort, KY: Gnomon.

Still, J. (1978). *River of Earth*. Lexington: University Press of Kentucky.

Wigginton, E. (1986). *Sometimes a Shining Moment*. Garden City, NY: Anchor Books.

What About the Skills? Shouldn't I Be Teaching Them?

BY BEVERLY WELLS
Squires Elementary
Fayette County Schools

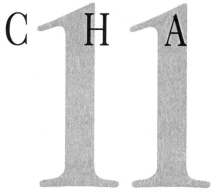

CHAPTER 11

Like many teachers of young children, I feel strongly that skills development is important for students at the primary level. Children not only need to learn fluency in writing and to enjoy reading, they also need "skills" for effective communication outside of school. So as I began my journey to develop a KERA primary program, my concerns about skills came with me. I knew that my students were having fun exploring, talking, painting, and manipulating as they worked in my classroom, but the ever-present question I faced was, "Are the skills being learned?"

I knew I had to trust that the changes I was making had worked for others and that the new practices were the best and most appropriate known. I also had to believe that a more open-ended continuous-progress approach would give all my students time to develop, and that within this four-year time frame of the primary program my students would be ready for the intermediate grades. I also knew that the development that would take place with my students would probably happen for me as well.

I have learned through experience that to become an effective teacher in a multi-age/multi-ability classroom I had to first confront my own philosophy and determine how well aligned it was with what I was doing. The security of curriculum guides and teacher's manuals was still available, but I was encouraged to use those guides only as resources as I designed a curriculum that would meet the needs of the primary children

in my classroom. This kind of freedom and choice would test my philosophy often as I began to make changes.

■ RISK-TAKING: THE WAY TO CHANGE

In Kentucky, as in most areas of the country, school districts spend thousands of dollars every four to six years on textbooks. Textbooks guide our curriculum. Someone outside my district had predetermined what skills the children in my classroom needed to know. The traditional approach to teaching reading, language arts, and spelling dictated that children were to be divided into ability groups, which became a caste system of sorts. Students who were most happy were those in the top reading group. The least happy were those who read in the low-group basals from the previous grade. Typically, the low group was comprised of the poor, the quiet, the linguistically different, and minorities. I was not happy with this system. At the time, my background in early childhood education prompted me to search for an alternative to this mundane and unfair approach to teaching. *Success in Reading and Writing* (Blackford & Cramer, 1980) had been around for about ten years. Based on research by Anne Adams, studies had shown that children were more apt to read and write information that they had generated by themselves.

I chose to use *Success in Reading and Writing,* a language experience program that uses the students' own language to teach reading and writing. This program helped me "bridge the gap" from a basal to a whole language approach. Further, using the children's own language as reading material helped them respect themselves as learners. It also got rid of the castelike system of ability groups. My district did require that the basal continue to be used in some way, so I chose to meet the requirement by using a reading contract where stories from basals were read at home, with parents signing the contract as the children completed each story.

The Success Program was a departure from the skills program of the basal because it used the students' language. Skill development continued to be an integral part of the program through such components as the phonics chart, self-selected spelling, and the integration of writing. I used a story chart to model writing and encourage vocabulary development. The program also had a research component that led to extensive student-generated writing. Independent reading material was self-selected.

I wondered if parents of my students would object to this change in our reading curriculum, but after an explanation at Open House, there were few concerns. The spelling component was explained, and the phonics charts were displayed and talked about with all parents present. Parents as a whole felt that this integrated approach opened the door for students to read without regard to grade level.

So my beginning attempt at risk taking had been established. With marker in hand, recording students' ideas in sentence or paragraph form, I taught skills as needed. When mistakes were made, they were corrected as a group. These demonstrations, done on a daily basis, were invaluable lessons for me as well as for my students.

■ WHOLE LANGUAGE: THE JOURNEY CONTINUES

My next "risk" was to add a literature-based approach to our reading program. Students self-selected books, took part in buddy reading, and shared with the class stories that were read at home. These activities brought me closer to a whole language approach in my teaching. Comprehension was now developed by comparing and contrasting stories rather than quizzing students after each story. I began to listen to students' responses to what they were reading and then to discuss their ideas.

I also began to use literature to integrate many areas of the curriculum through such activities as

- collecting data from a story to complete a graph (math)
- choosing spelling words from a story (spelling/word study)
- using a pattern/format of a book to write about another topic (language arts)

Students soon suggested possible projects from books, and many lively discussions were held. I valued all responses; all efforts were celebrated; all student work was displayed and (at times) published in our classroom newsletter. I discovered that giving children permission to become risk takers was important as well. I found that valuing student suggestions encouraged them to become comfortable expressing their ideas. They discovered that there were many and varied ways to respond. In such an environment, individual ideas flowed. Thinking this way made me realize how far I had come from the days when the right answer was more important than any kind of self-expression by students, and when the most important thing to remember about teaching was to take the grade book with me during a fire drill!

■ INTEGRATION: USING THEMES

The next part of my journey was to integrate the curriculum more fully. Integrating the curriculum through the use of themes was time consuming, but not difficult. The research that I did to develop the units and activities was a learning experience in itself. Recently our study of folklore led to discussions of the country of origin of each story. The country was identified after much speculation, based upon clues, and then located on a map or globe. The dialogue about what makes folklore interesting led to discussions and illustrations of different versions of familiar tall tales, legends, folktales, and fairy tales. Reading, writing, listening, speaking, geography, and history all came together as we focused on the content of a theme.

I discovered that through thematic studies, broad concepts tie into the students' lives, and that higher levels of thinking occur when children make connections. For example, in a study of movement our team of five teachers found that we could develop thirteen to fourteen smaller units such as time, age, music, numbers, and insects, to name just a

few. Students were able to connect real-life experiences to the more global theme of movement and to demonstrate their understandings through music or math or kinesthetically.

Teaching in this way began to shift my focus from skills to learner outcomes, to what I wanted children to demonstrate. When I began to focus teaching toward a specific outcome, the question, "How will the skills be learned in a multi-age classroom?" was answered. Skills contribute to the students' demonstrations (outcomes), but my focus has shifted from isolated skills to the application and development of skills through the outcome. I now ask myself, "What do I want my students to learn as a result of their participation in this unit of study?" Focusing on learner outcomes directs my thinking and concern for skill development beyond what were often cute, isolated activities that had little relationship to the application and purpose of the skills. I now ask students to engage in *real* activities that have a realistic relationship to what they are studying. I teach and monitor skill development as a way of improving students' performances.

For example, after reading about Rosa Parks's difficulty riding a city bus in Montgomery, Alabama, in the early 1960s, students were asked to write and perform a play, poem, or song about how she must have felt after having worked all day and being asked to give up her seat on the bus to a white passenger.

Working in cooperative groups enabled everyone to participate and

Working in cooperative groups enabled everyone to participate and complete the task. In this instance, students were asked to demonstrate learning through written as well as oral communication.

My goal was for all students to demonstrate through a cooperative task that they had learned the contributions this very quiet woman had made to our society. I was also able to assess oral and written language skills.

■ SO WHAT ABOUT THE SKILLS?

When I taught the traditional way, I tried to make my language arts block as interesting as possible for students who weren't reading with me. Poems, plays, and games were utilized to make reading more fun. I do not think teachers intentionally try to make children unhappy in school, but I could see the unhappiness on my students' faces each day when we began yet another segment approach to teaching and learning. Because *Success in Reading and Writing* lent itself to integration in the language arts area, the natural progression was to try to incorporate as much writing across the other curriculum areas as possible. I soon began to use social studies themes in the research and writing modules. I found that giving students many opportunities to think about what actually happens in our world on a daily basis helped relieve them of the feeling of being boxed in when responding to an open-ended question.

The opportunity to teach *Success*, with parents' support, led to two years of change in what was then a traditional third grade class. Students became less concerned about one-answer questions; journal writing became routine; students wrote across the curriculum; and, importantly, students were not assigned to reading groups based on any particular skill.

With these experiences as a foundation, I felt confident about making further changes in creating a whole language classroom and in teaching more thematically. And I learned to review the teaching of skills from a new perspective. As I talk with other teachers about developing their primary classrooms, I encourage them to begin with what's comfortable, observe and learn from children's responses, and be open to change. Everyone can benefit.

REFERENCE

Blackford, B. J., & Cramer, B. (1980). *Success in Reading and Writing*. New York: Scott, Foresman.

SECTION 4

REFORM AS A SHARED ENDEAVOR

As a parent and community member, I have watched the transition to nongraded primary with a critical eye. I have twin daughters who survived the "traditional" classroom and are doing well as sixth graders. Now my youngest is being taught in a flexible classroom environment where she is encouraged to learn problem-solving strategies and work in peer-group situations as part of the daily routine. Education is important to my husband and me. I was concerned about proposed changes in the primary school. I wanted to find out all I could about the benefits of this new program for my child.

Jeannie Bass, Parent
Silver Grove Elementary

In this section, the voices of teachers, parents, and school administrators involved with the primary program are heard. The authors of the following three chapters all agree that it takes a variety of people to make reform of this scale work. These chapters describe the struggles and strategies in getting teachers, parents, community members, school staff, school boards, and school administrators involved in reform efforts.

WHAT A DIFFERENCE A YEAR MAKES

BY CATHERINE PILLOW, SHERRY FIELD,
VERNELL DEVINE, AND WENDY FURMAN
Mason-Corinth Elementary
Grant County Schools

CHAPTER 12

■ FAMILY TIME . . . IN THE BEGINNING

In the beginning we put our children together, gave directions, and expected a finished product from each child. We were more concerned with spending weekly "family time" together than with the educational outcomes. But now we are able to allow the children to make choices and be responsible learners. How did this happen?

"Family time" consisted of three teachers who combined classes for one to three hours per week. This meshed six- and seven-year-olds with the seven- and eight-year-olds, who were in the traditional first, second, and third grades. In our classes we had an age span of six to ten years.

We enjoyed combining classes, but it began to wear us out trying to achieve finished products. It was a chore barking our instructions to seventy children making paper soldiers as a follow-up to our field trip to the "Nutcracker" ballet. There had to be a better way.

■ FAMILY TIME . . . AFTER WE LEARNED THE HARD WAY

The science lab buzzed with the activity of seventy primary students. The children were involved in a family activity leading to the culmination of a thematic study of birds. They were divided into ten cooperative learning groups and asked to answer one of the following questions:

1. What do you know about birds?

2. What do you know about owls?

3. What do you know about penguins?

Each group had been instructed to devise a method for displaying and presenting their information to the remaining groups. The information was to be displayed on a large piece of bulletin board paper.

While the children worked, Catherine asked them what they knew about owl pellets. She jotted anecdotal notes about specific students. These records were kept on each student in lieu of grades and enabled us to see in a much more complete way how the children had grown. They told us not only how the children were doing academically but also how they were interacting with peers, an important component in KERA. Meanwhile, Sherry monitored several groups to keep them on task. Wendy talked with a group about a penguin web they had constructed. Finally, the children were ready to present their information to the family. As each group presented, we were able to make valuable notes about communication, listening, and organizational skills. As we evaluated the process our students had made, we also assessed the quality of our family instructional activities. This assessment helped us realize that we had made great strides in planning for and implementing family activities.

■ CATHERINE AND SHERRY LOOK BACK

Some teachers and schools were wary of KERA. It was no different at our school. In the spring of 1992, major changes were taking place at Mason-Corinth Elementary. We had just moved from two old buildings into a brand-new facility. We were also informed that major administrative changes would be taking place, and the staff was unsure of their placements for the next year. Everyone knew that there was the possibility of being transferred to another grade level or another building. These uncertainties made it nearly impossible to focus on the important task of preparing for the primary program.

In early May it was announced that we would have a new principal, and in July we were given our assignments for the 1992-93 school year. Our primary unit consisted of three teams of kindergartens that integrated with the primary classrooms for one to two hours per week.

Each team was made up of one six- and seven-year-old classroom and one seven- and eight-year-old classroom. Even though we were relieved to have our assignments, we were overwhelmed with what lay before us. Time constraints became a real problem. Schedules had to be set, room assignments needed to be altered to provide ease of movement within families, and classrooms had to be rearranged to meet the needs of the students. Students needed to be placed, and parents needed to be notified of classroom assignments. Thematic units had to be developed, materials ordered, and team strategies planned. We had to make up for lost time.

In early August we attended a primary institute on developing assessment instruments, instructional units, and classroom management strategies. This greatly increased our comfort level for implementing the primary program. The central office staff was supportive and provided opportunities for training in "Box-It, Bag-It," thematic units, and whole language.

As the beginning of school approached, the search for an assistant principal began. Our principal had hoped to find a candidate who could provide leadership and expertise in the primary field. The position was filled with someone with a strong knowledge base in the primary program and fourteen years' teaching experience in varied teaching assignments in grades one through twelve. Our principal and assistant principal proved to make a great team, and they helped ease the transition and provided positive reinforcement for the primary staff. Through both difficult and easy times, we consistently found ourselves saying to one another, "We are so lucky to have leadership and support from the administration. We could not have made it this far without their help." Our success was largely due to that support.

After school began, the administration realized that the primary classes were overcrowded and decided to hire another teacher. After interviewing several candidates, the decision was made to hire Wendy, an intern with an elementary certification in K-4. The members of the team of teachers shared similar philosophies and were able to use individual strengths to successfully work together to meet the needs of our primary family.

■ WENDY JOINS THE TEAM

Two weeks into the school year, while I was still a substitute teacher, the principal offered me a permanent position. I became the newest faculty member at Mason-Corinth Elementary. Then reality set in. Someone said, "Well, this is your classroom!" I looked around and saw nothing! I panicked. I did not know what I needed, what other teachers had to offer, or what my limits were. Yet our wonderful administration helped save my first year of teaching. Whatever I asked for, I received. From the first day, I felt comfortable with our principal and assistant principal. That was extremely important to me and the main reason I survived my first year.

On my first official day, the assistant principal took me to the local Wal-Mart and told me to buy whatever I needed. This came as a complete surprise. Little did I know that there was something called "start-up" money.

My next major meeting was with other teachers. This was probably the strongest support that the administration could have shown me. I was really lucky that the three of us meshed so well. Since we had eliminated textbooks and ability groupings, my family of teachers became an invaluable resource in my teaching. They shared with me their experience, knowledge, materials, and encouragement. I could not have been put in a better situation and will always be grateful to those four people.

My class consisted of children whose ages ranged from six to ten. Since I was the only teacher to have this age span, I was given a lot of sympathy. As a first-year teacher, I used to say that ignorance was bliss. There was definitely some truth in that statement. I had no real experience in a traditional classroom, so I did not have anything to compare with the new experience I was encountering. Even so, the first two months were awful. I smiled at school, and then went home and cried. My husband either encouraged me or urged me to quit, depending on my mood that day. I often called my sister, a teacher in the same county, and she too gave me unlimited support. As the year went on, I found that I was not the only person feeling overwhelmed and tired. My greatest fear was that I could not meet the needs of my students. Sometimes people need to hear that they are on the right track. My principal and assistant principal are such giving people and provided me with much-needed encouragement. What surprised me was that they did not do it only when I had that look on my face but gave me a daily boost of positive reinforcement and support.

■ VERNELL'S CONTRIBUTION

When I received the phone call from the principal at Mason-Corinth telling me I was the candidate his committee had selected for the assistant principal's position at Mason-Corinth, I took the job without the slightest hesitation. I did not know any of the circumstances surrounding Mason-Corinth. I did not realize that the principal would also be new to the school, but I was so impressed by his candor and openness that I knew we could work well together.

As an assistant principal, I assumed that one of my responsibilities would be student discipline. However, the principal had other plans for me. He had checked resumes for a candidate who had a strong background in primary education and involvement in training and professional workshops. He was searching for an individual who could be an effective instructional leader for the primary program.

I had been involved in many aspects of the primary program in Woodford County. As I began my employment at Mason-Corinth, I was asked to devote most of my time to the primary program. The teachers were cordial and receptive to suggestions. In the first month of school, I prepared packets of materials of strategies they might try. I spent a great deal of time talking with them about what they needed and the most effective way I could help. They gave me several suggestions, and from these suggestions my role in this program evolved.

Even though some teachers were further along than others, all of them were giving their heart and soul to their profession and needed all the extra support I could give. Although each team had forty-five minutes a day for planning, they said they needed more. I developed a plan where I would be in each team's primary classroom thirty minutes per week. The teachers used this time for extra planning within their family. While in the classrooms, I used whole language activities to further enhance the students' learning. I realized that this time was invaluable to the teachers, and I rescheduled if I had to be out of the building.

I spent many hours writing a proposal for a grant that would help teachers become more effective in integrating the curriculum in the areas of mathematics and science and also develop more strategies for whole language teaching. We were fortunate to receive the grant, and in January were able to have two professors from Northern Kentucky University, Dr. Lynne Smith, a literacy specialist, and Dr. Linda Sheffield, a mathematics specialist, come to our school and provide assistance to our teachers in a workshop setting. Substitutes were provided in the classrooms as part of the grant funding. This allowed teachers to gain knowledge and expertise during school hours rather than at the end of a school day when they were exhausted and unable to focus their thoughts. Through this grant, we were also able to visit other programs and compare our program to theirs. Our teachers began to realize that they were headed in the right direction for full implementation of the primary school.

I could never have asked for a more satisfying beginning to my administrative career. I have had the total support of the principal, the teachers, and the parents of the students at Mason-Corinth Elementary. We have had fun this year working together and growing as a team. It shows in the way we handle the day-to-day situations of primary school. What is most important is that the children are truly enjoying learning, and after all, isn't that the way it should be?

■ WHAT WORKED

We were fortunate to be in a situation in which we had the freedom to experiment without constraint. Failures were met with disappointment, but also with feelings of having learned something valuable. We were allowed to pause midstream, re-evaluate, and start over, if necessary. This freedom made it possible to grow professionally and to fine-tune our program.

Initially we were concerned about creating developmentally appropriate activities to meet the needs of a multi-age/multi-level group. Thematic units helped alleviate some of our concerns. We were able to work together to develop units that interested our students and parents. These units were also excellent tools for home-school communication. Parents were encouraged to spend some time at school and to share their expertise. The use of thematic units and consistent correspondence with parents helped all of us feel ownership of the work being done. Even though we had great success teaching thematically, we were not pressured to make sure that every piece of our day coincided with that time. If math would not fit into our theme, then we would make do with a regular math lesson.

Whole language teaching, including a focus on the writing process, has been most beneficial to our students' progress. Extensive daily writing helped students in their fluency and clarity as writers and aided their language development. The children also enjoyed having their choice of reading materials. They became more willing to take chances, and they did not suffer the embarrassment of labeling caused by traditional basal groups.

In our attempts to serve a multi-level group, mathematics was initially a great challenge. It was difficult to let go of the notion that children should be working on a particular grade level. We knew from the beginning that our math instruction needed to be very different from traditional textbook instruction. Knowing this, we pulled from one another's education. We used manipulatives daily in each of our classrooms, and our students had access to these materials when needed.

An example of success teaching math came for Wendy near the end of the year. She used an overhead projector, overhead fraction pieces, a shoe box with money, and the minds of the children. Here are the concepts and methods she used. Keep in mind that she was teaching six- to ten-year-olds.

1. The children had to guess how much money was in the box. Each guess cost them 1/8 of a pie. At first the children would guess whole amounts ("Is it fifty cents?"). Then they caught on to more than/less than amounts.

They would say, "Is it *more than* $1.00?" In this one step, the concepts of fractions and greater than/less than were utilized, as were their critical thinking skills.

2. After they guessed the amount, Wendy told them the number of coins in the box. They then had to tell her the *combination* of coins (two nickels, one dime, and so on) that were in the shoe box. She divided the class into six groups of four students to work out the problem. Each group had coins, pencil, and paper to solve the problem. This activity used both the children's critical thinking skills and group skills.

Each day became a new challenge for the children. They wanted to lessen the number of fraction pieces it took to guess the amount in the shoe box. The children became more and more efficient at guessing and figuring out the amount. The students who were best at this task were those who were six and seven years old at the beginning of the school year.

Our varied math programs quickly convinced us that multiage/multi-level grouping could work. All of our students were able to feel success at this time. Soon even six-year-olds were doing extended math equations, understanding place value, using multiplication and division, and trying to outdo the older students during this nonthreatening time.

As we became more comfortable with the concept of the primary program, we were able to focus more and more on developmentally appropriate activities. With the support of our principal and assistant principal, our primary program had advanced rapidly. We have been afforded shared planning time, extensive training, support, and the freedom to make professional choices.

We realize that we have a long way to go, but we believe that the key to an effective program is to never be satisfied with how things are and to keep reaching for the stars. We believe in the KERA philosophy that all students can learn, and our goal is to help them.

A Principal's Perspective for Educational Reform

BY JOE JACOVINO
Camden Station Elementary
Oldham County Schools

CHAPTER 13

KERA—Kentucky Early Retirement Action or Kentucky Education Reform Act? When the state passed the reform act, many speculated about what the acronym really meant. At our school, we feel it meant reforming what was basically an out-of-date educational system. There is an extensive amount of literature dealing with education reform. This chapter will deal with three key areas of implementation of the reform at the school level. First, what resources, both within and outside education, could be utilized during implementation? Second, what steps can be taken to bring the school stakeholders into the process of change? Third, how do schools implement systemic reform?

Camden Station Elementary opened in 1988 as a cooperative learning/collaborative teaching school. The income levels of our students' parents range from zero to about six hundred thousand a year. We offer a wide range of programs, from collaborative special education to gifted. Our school has a capacity of 550 children, from five-year-olds to fifth grade. Our staff come from a variety of backgrounds and states. The average number of years they have taught is seven. My training was in New England, and I taught for several years in New York and Kentucky. My leadership style has been described as interpersonal.

■ PROFESSIONAL DEVELOPMENT RESOURCES

In order to be successful, a school, through its principal, must stay in touch with the educational currents that are constantly flowing around it. Prior to the reform act of 1990, our school implemented several new ideas that we felt would improve student outcomes. Primarily this involved cooperative learning and collaborative teaching. Helping teachers effectively implement any new program requires a tremendous amount of staff development, and, in turn, a tremendous amount of resources, both in money and time. Staff development became my main vehicle to help overcome resistance to change. I had to make sure all staff, even those with over twenty years of teaching, could make the shift. I firmly believe that a successful school needs its senior as well as its junior staff members. We needed to all have our oars in the water at the same time if this ship was going to move!

To meet and plan appropriate staff development we needed to come up with a budget, a source of funding, and time. We decided to seek the support of the school's stakeholder, the Parent Teacher Organization. When we approached this organization, we made a simple proposal. We asked, "Do you want to directly influence the education of your children?" The answer was a resounding "Yes!" In order to do this, we asked that they include a budget item for the next school term that included staff development. We asked for $3,000. We explained that buying equipment was great, as were all the other "extras," but the need to re-educate the staff was now more critical than ever before.

With the P.T.O. money and money from the board, we were able to put together a comprehensive school-based staff development program. Our staff visited schools and districts in and out of state. (Two of the best we found were The Key School in Indianapolis and Wickliffe, outside Columbus, Ohio.) The teachers observed and learned what worked and what did not. They attended workshops in Illinois, Ohio, Tennessee, Georgia, as well as Kentucky. Staff members who had years of experience were as open to attending out-of-state workshops as the rest of the teachers. They were as willing as the rest of us to see the role of the teacher change from being the "sage on the stage to the guide on the side." Each staff member was required to share with all of us what she or he had learned. From these visits, we learned about cooperative learning, learning modalities, grouping and tracking practices, business partnerships, technology, and wellness for staff and students.

As staff returned from the various visits and workshops, we passed information along to parents. Several times during the various outings, parents were part of the teams. They were partners in the reformation of our school. Over the last three years, our school has spent approximately $23,000 on staff development. While this is a great amount of money, in our opinion it was still not enough!

Our extensive research, our visits to nationally recognized schools, and our intensive staff development provided a framework from which to develop our new primary program.

One advantage we had was our board of education. Our superintendent and assistants were all eager for us to explore and try options. The board gave us great freedom to start the implementation process. This chapter could not be written without acknowledging the tremendous amount of work and support from our assistant superintendent, Dr. Charleen McAuliffe. She organized committees on assessing and reporting student achievement, worked to find sites to visit, recommended further research to read, and attended staff development activities and school visits with the staff and parents.

The resources available to schools for staff development have gotten better and more useful. We discovered that how a school uses staff development to focus on student outcomes and teacher education is as important as finding the resources. We used our professional development to revise our report cards and the way we conduct parent conferences and even became more selective in workshops we attend. Our report cards now are more parent friendly, and our parent conferences revolve around outcome-based educational goals.

In the spring of 1992 a committee of district teachers and administrators explored the option of taking five instructional days for continued staff development. After attending a three-day session on outcome-based education and reviewing the literature from the High Success Network, the committee recommended to the entire staff and board that the five-day development option be taken.

The staff development committee's desire was to work to foster communication by the district teachers in both a horizontal and lateral way. Staff from elementary schools that sent children to a particular middle school met with staff from the middle and high schools. All parents, community members, and higher education people who wished to attend the workshop were given that opportunity. The staff at each school met, and then teams within each school met. The purpose was to find out: Where are we in implementing the reform? What is outcome-based education? How will the reform affect student learning? How will we as teachers and schools use this staff development to better meet the needs of all our students? Follow-up sessions were scheduled for the following year. This allowed us to get educated, use what we learned, and then assess the learning that had taken place.

■ BRINGING IN THE STAKEHOLDERS

Are we building the plane as we're flying it? Many of us have heard this statement, and we realized from the beginning that in order to accomplish the reforms successfully, we needed the support of *all* the stakeholders.

One of our first tasks was to identify who the stakeholders were. As we worked through the process of identifying these people or groups, we became increasingly aware that the list needed to be as inclusive as possible. The standard list includes teachers, parents, and students. We extended it, bringing in the board of education, central office administrators, businesses, retired parents, and classified staff.

The school guidance counselor also played an integral role in the entire process, a role that was possibly more vital than that of the principal. We will see later how vital it was and continues to be.

A school public relations plan has always been required in our county. We decided early on that we would give the community as much information as we had. When possible, we shared information as soon as it was available. Our P.T.O. sponsored "KERA Nights." As a part of this program, we met with parents and explained what was happening in the legislature. When the law passed, we started to hold informational meetings to help explain to our community why we were going to have to change.

Our topics for these meetings ranged from "What is KERA?" and "What, Me Worry?" to "Into the 21st Century." At one of the first meetings we ran into a buzzsaw of questions: "Why are you changing what you are doing? You have been so successful and now you're doing this junk?" "What happened to the grades? Are we to guess how our children are doing?" "What about my gifted child—is he just going to be teaching the slower children all day?" and even, "Why do educators keep trying new things on our children? First it was the *new math,* then it was something else. Give it a rest! Go back to the basics!" Needless to say, it was a very interesting and stressful time for all of us.

At the meetings we used overheads and VCR tapes provided by the state department of education. The sessions were helpful to a majority of parents. But parents still wanted to see KERA in action. Yet inviting them to visit the classrooms presented many problems. We found that a great many wanted to visit, and it appeared that most parents were looking for negatives. We then decided that it would be best to limit visits to certain days and times so as not to interrupt instruction. During the final "KERA Night" we heard parent comments that spanned the entire range of feelings about the reform, from, "Don't do it, the legislature will change their minds about it anyway" to, "This is the greatest thing I have seen in school for my child."

Change always causes some stress. Massive change can cause massive stress. This is where the counselor comes in. Many times parents or staff for one reason or another needed an "outside" opinion. Our community had a difficult time accepting the change because of our high academic successes in the previous years. The questions continued: "Is this really going to work?" "Will this be better for our children?" These questions were most usually directed to the counselor, Ms. Denise White, known as a child advocate at our building. Parents see her as the bridge between teachers and the administrator.

KERA Nights extended into the homes of "host families." Many times the counselor, a teacher, and I would visit a subdivision, and the host families would invite the neighborhood in to ask questions. This certainly helped communication in many areas. The parents were given a chance to ask more detailed questions; the teachers heard concerns

that they communicated to the school; and the administrators got a chance to be accessible to the public.

After the informational meetings came the "hands-on" meetings. Teachers were given staff-development training by the state so that they could give parents a "feel" for what was happening in the learning process. We decided to have KERA "Math Nights" in which teachers and parents participate in the same kinds of conceptually based hands-on mathematics that their children were receiving each day. We sent invitations to all guardians and business groups and placed invitations in doctors' and real estate offices. Our P.T.O. officers were behind all our efforts and attended every meeting and neighborhood session. During these KERA "Math Nights," the M&M's flowed, the unifix cubes were counted, and our parents and staff were given money and asked to plan twenty meals for the week. *They* then told *us* what other areas of instruction could be integrated into this math lesson. We heard shouts of "nutrition," "reading," and "geography." Our business representatives were most impressed. We heard comments like "children should become 'generalists' and NOT be trained in specifics. We'll train them in specifics if you give them the big picture." Our evenings were rewarding for all. Teachers felt more appreciated for what they do, and parents had a better understanding of how mathematics instruction reflected real life. The feedback from all these meetings helped shape our approach to what was happening and would happen in the classroom. We were open to trying new ideas from parents as well as staff. At one informational meeting a group of parents asked if we could have siblings in the same classroom. My immediate reaction was no. After we discussed the idea, we decided that our response was based on what our staff had always done. We remembered the saying, "If you always do what you've always done, you'll always get what you've always gotten." We decided to give the idea of siblings in the same room a try, with some restrictions. If the teacher or parent felt the arrangement was not working, then either could request a change of placement. To their credit, our staff does not have a problem with "turf." They do not look on a change of placement as a loss for themselves. They are secure in their professionalism. When it comes time to make a decision, they always make it based on what they feel is best for the child. This confidence was achieved through school visits, conferences, and staff development activities in working out all the concerns and issues associated with KERA.

How do the classified staff play into the reform movement? Whether it is at the supermarket, a ball game, or a gas station, all staff come in contact with the community at some time. It is important that they be able to communicate what is happening in the school. They are an integral part of what we are attempting to do. The cafeteria this year has been inundated with students doing cooking math; the custodians have been giving math lessons on area and perimeter; the secretaries have listened to enough young authors to fill a library; and the instructional assistants work hand in glove with the teachers.

A new respect for the classified staff has come about since their inclusion in the process of learning. Children look at these folks differently than before. No longer are they seen in isolated roles as the cleaning person or the cook. To be of real value, learning must be shown to be useful. What better way to do this in the school setting than by drawing on the people who use math, reading, and writing every day? Our primary children worked with the cafeteria in baking for the day (measuring and weighing). Our intermediate students helped the custodian measure for carpet and cork stripping.

Finally, the central office has been part of our school reform. With site-based, participatory management, or any of the hybrids, comes a certain amount of decentralization. Bringing the decision making to the members closest to the problem is a move in the right direction, but it also has its drawbacks. No matter how one communicates with the public, they are apt to see the school board as the ultimate arbiter. If a parent does not like what he or she hears at the school level, the next step is often to call the board. The call will be directed to the person in the central office closest to the area of concern. How much better for those involved in education to know what is going on at the school and have input into the process. These educators are a vital link in the communication process. They usually have daily contact with the superintendent and contacts with board of education members. They can communicate the goals of the schools, help resolve parents' concerns, and help bring the two together. They serve as a lightning rod in many cases and can be most helpful in getting exemptions to policy, so the school can try to develop different approaches. For example, one parent wanted to know if eliminating grades was "legal." He asked why one school was allowed to eliminate grades while another has not. The central office was a great help in reassuring this parent that the changes at the schools are legal and good for the children and that the education of his child is still being monitored. The more the central office knows about what is going on at a school, the more reassuring and helpful it can be to *both* school and community.

■ NOW, LET'S GO FOR IT!

Lastly, there are repercussions the school and staff can expect during reform. We have educated the staff, communicated with the central office, worked with the parent group, held meetings to inform the various school publics, put items in the newsletter, sent home informational sheets, and thought we were ready to go. Were we ever wrong!

Hindsight showed us the need for budgeting for materials, working to get even more parents into the building and classrooms to see the process in action, and somehow getting information to those parents who, for whatever reasons, did not get the information, attend the sessions, or hear about the changes being implemented. These were critical areas that had to be given a great deal of attention.

While trying to put this reform into place, teachers needed time for trial and error. Yet, many times parents wanted to observe and be in the classrooms immediately after school opened. So we needed a compromise. We arrived at a balance that met the needs of all concerned. We decided that the counselor and principal would answer as many questions as possible from parents. No classroom visits took place until the second semester. Appointments were set up with the principal first, and the following day one-hour visits were arranged with a teacher.

With this plan, the visits did not interrupt the lessons. At the end of each visit, if time permitted, the teacher would answer the visitor's questions. The visitor then met with me or the counselor and was able to ask further questions and get additional information and feedback.

The need for visits came from the parents' discomfort with the unknown. On one level the staff understood this. However, the stress with dealing with unknown visitors was apparent. We decided early on that we would not be on "show." We would do what we always did and try to be as helpful as possible. At first, the staff often felt the parents did not trust them. Yet it was apparently not a matter of mistrust but more of curiosity about what was going on in the classroom.

Stress was also caused by an increased work load. With the change of instruction came more work in the classroom, more individual assessment, more conferences (phone and in person), and less material being sent home. Parents had liked the traditional dittos that had been sent home because they felt these gave them a gauge of what was going on in their child's education. Without this frame of reference, many parents felt they had lost touch with how their child was progressing. More frequent conferences, notes, and phone calls, along with classroom visits, helped alleviate some of the stress parents were feeling.

■ FUTURE IMPLEMENTATION: STILL GROWING AND CHANGING

The next phase of education reform that we needed to implement was *kindergarten integration*. We called together a committee of teachers and parents called the Primary Design Committee. We had staff from each team, including art, music, physical education, special education, and guidance.

The committee worked hard through some very stressful times. They had to decide whether to integrate five-year-olds all day, part of a day, or just a few hours of each day. After five months the committee reached a consensus. We decided to go with programs for five- and six-year-olds and for seven- and eight-year-olds. The next step was to get the word out about the forthcoming changes. A series of evening meetings was scheduled at which I gave overviews of how we arrived at this stage of evolution in the primary program. We then broke into about ten groups, with two staff and parents at each group to answer questions.

These sessions with parents were received very well. The parents were excited and supportive. At this time, however, we had just learned that we may be facing a severe cut in the formula for state funding for schools. If that happened, our all-day primary program would be canceled, and we would have to look at other options. The old adage that the more things change the more they stay the same certainly seemed true in this case.

I could not end this chapter without expressing a strong personal belief that in spite of all the questions, concerns, and changes that have affected education in Kentucky, I firmly believe that the legislature has done a great thing. The children will be better educated and more productive citizens. The resource we now need more than anything else is *time*. Time to let the reforms work and take root. Time to assess and re-evaluate. We need at least the rest of the nineties to make sure that the Kentucky Education Reform Act has created strong pilots to fly this new plane.

PARTNERSHIPS FOR LEARNERS

BY JEANNIE BASS, LINDA BIBEE,
AND DIANA HEIDELBERG
Silver Grove Elementary
Silver Grove Schools

CHAPTER 14

"David and I have a great puppet show we made up."

"I'll ask Susan how to spell Kentucky."

"Can I read this book to the class?"

"I can count to l00. Want to hear me?"

"We are writing a book together. Can we type it on the computer?"

"Is it time to go home already?"

The voices of children are heard throughout Kentucky, and within the primary school their voices are excited about learning. They face each new challenge with confidence. The children feel success each day they are in school.

Behind these voices of children are the voices of parents, teachers, and administrators, voices that form the framework on which the children rely. These voices are heard in this chapter as they trace the evolution of the primary program at Silver Grove Elementary School. They are united on some issues and in disagreement on others. There is, however, a respect for the worth of all voices and their right to be heard.

Silver Grove works because the staff, students, and parents want to make it a success. The representative voices in this chapter include those of Jeannie Bass, a parent with three children who attend Silver Grove; Diana Heidelberg, the principal; and a primary teacher, Linda Bibee (who speaks in the collective "we" to include her colleagues Catherine Caudill and Becky Haas). Each of these different voices contributes a unique perspective on the primary program. As a whole we are proud of our efforts and eager to share our experiences with this innovative program.

Diana, the Principal:

Silver Grove is located in Campbell County, Kentucky. It lies about five miles east of Cincinnati, Ohio. Incorporated in 1950, it has a population of 1,300. Silver Grove School is an independent K-12 school system with two sessions of preschool and four low-incidence handicap units. Our total enrollment is 300 students. Although some of the students come from neighboring cities, most live in town, and all are from lower- and middle-class families.

Keeping the school open and independent has been a challenge to the community. There are those who believe that a school this small cannot operate efficiently. Those involved with Silver Grove Schools believe that it offers a sense of community and family at a time when these are becoming rare commodities. The people who support our school have fought to keep it open. In the process many of them have participated as part of a transition team for the nongraded primary.

Jeannie Bass, a Parent:

As a parent and community member, I have watched the transition to nongraded primary with a critical eye. I have twin daughters who survived the "traditional" classroom and are doing well as sixth graders. Now my youngest daughter is being taught in a flexible classroom environment where she is encouraged to learn problem-solving strategies and work in peer-group situations as part of the daily routine. Education is important to my husband and me. I was concerned about proposed changes in the primary school. I wanted to find out all I could about the benefits of this new program for my child.

Linda Bibee and the Primary Team:

Spring is a time of rebirth in nature's world. In the spring of 1990, it was also a time of rebirth and new thinking by our primary teachers. After reading much about the new KERA programs, especially the concept of primary school, we felt a need to experience this new concept for ourselves. Catherine Caudill and I, teaching first and second graders, worked together to plan a unit on the properties of matter (i.e., whether objects float or sink, are hard or soft, smooth or rough). We decided to teach our children together. Later in the spring, we introduced a unit on nutrition to the students and included a class of eight- and nine-year-olds in a multi-age/multi-ability situation with six-, seven-, and eight-year-olds.

After that brief glimpse into multi-age/multi-ability teaching, we finished the school year knowing that we had begun teaching in a new and different way. We knew that we were going to like the new classroom. As we planned for the next year we formed our team—Linda Bibee, a twenty-two-year veteran of second, third and fourth grade; Catherine Caudill, a sixteen-year veteran of kindergarten, remedial reading, first, second, and sixth grade; and Becky Haas, a first-year teacher. What a variety of people with different ideas and experiences! We began to plan for the 1991-92 school year by arranging our groups. In the morning the children went to grade-level classes. During homeroom time and afternoons we grouped children heterogeneously in multi-age/multi-ability classrooms.

Jeannie Bass, a Parent:

When Alanna first went to kindergarten (before the nongraded primary), she came home and did not offer anything about what had taken place in the classroom. At times I would just pass this off as her not being able to "get a word in edgewise" because of her two very vocal older sisters. I soon realized that this was not the case. According to her teacher, Alanna participated in class, cooperated well with her classmates, completed assignments on time, and seemed to look at education as many people look at a job. They put in their eight hours a day to the best of their ability, and when they come home, they're home, leaving work behind. This was Alanna. She enjoyed school and did well, but she did not bring it home with her.

169

Meanwhile, my twin daughters came home every day just bubbling with school news. Alanna did not share this enthusiasm. To me, Alanna's lack of enthusiasm was very sad. "Next year will be better," I told myself.

Linda Bibee and the Primary Team:

Summertime: vacations, leisure, sleeping in—but not for us! We continued to read more on the primary school concept. We attended seminars and workshops. We bounced ideas off each other, our spouses, and our families. That summer it seemed that our minds were on the upcoming school year and the monumental change that was going to take place in the classroom. We decided to pursue the same theme throughout the whole primary block. Trees would be a theme that could encompass all aspects of the curriculum throughout the school year. We laid aside the textbooks, relying on trade books, whole language techniques, math manipulatives, hands-on science, maps, globes, field trips, and walking trips about town to complete curriculum requirements. Our biggest asset in making these changes was our principal, Diana Heidelberg. As a former classroom teacher herself, she understood our needs and let us make decisions for ourselves.

Diana, the Principal:

The primary teachers embraced the tenets of the primary program so readily. They were enthusiastic about the changes. They wanted to accept the challenges and overcome them. The administrative branch of the school found that empowerment of the teachers was the key to success in the primary program. We enthusiastically supported all the teachers' ideas. We let them make plans and change them if necessary. Dictating policy from the top does not work with primary programs; the teachers need to feel ownership in the program.

Linda Bibee and the Primary Team:

As the summer drew to a close, panic set in, but we knew we were well prepared and ready to make the best of this new situation. We advertised around town that we would have a parent-teacher meeting the week before school started to inform parents of the new changes. We had heard rumors that some parents did not want the primary program implemented. They were afraid that their children's needs would not be met. We wanted to assure these parents as much as possible. The night of the meeting arrived, and some of the parents who were opposed to the ideas of the primary program were there. Other parents also were there, and we were not sure of their position on the issue. As the meeting began, the teachers of the primary school were introduced, and we watched a video from the Kentucky Department of Education showing real children at work in a successful program. After the video we presented our program to the parents and then opened the floor for questions and comments. One parent asked, "Will my children be running around the room from center to center? What if they choose only play activities all day?" Others asked, "How can you teach without textbooks?" "Will the older children lose valuable learning time if they have to help the younger ones?"

We assured the parents that the primary school promotes structure just like in the regular classroom. We talked about small-group instruction with children who had the same needs. We talked about peer tutoring and its benefits to both the tutor and the learner. And we talked about the importance of children choosing their own individual work. The subject of report cards was brought up. We had already received board approval to issue narrative reports every three weeks. Some parents voiced concerns that their children needed traditional letter grades; we responded with reassurances that the parents would know more about their children's progress through a narrative report than through letter grades.

The meeting ended. We felt that the parents left with more confidence than when they arrived and that most would be supportive of the program.

Jeannie Bass, a Parent:

I understand where parents are coming from in their questions and concerns. Why don't we receive report cards with letter grades? I also worry about my child being grouped with older children. But I don't feel these concerns should be our total focus. Many children who thrive in traditional classrooms are learners and will learn in any situation. The exciting thing about the reform is that no learner is limited. Children have the opportunity to learn more than ever before.

Another positive discovery I made about the primary school is the de-emphasis on competition. My older girls are always competing, especially because they are twins. This is encouraged in the traditional grading system. It is easy for them to compare A's to A's and B's to B's and to decide who did better.

On the other hand, assessment in the primary classroom is individual and is not conducive to comparisons. The narrative reporting method is a positive step toward parent involvement. Because the report deals specifically with my children's progress and achievement, I can see the strengths and weaknesses in plain language. I know where my daughters need help. This type of assessment tells me much more than a letter grade. I feel more encouraged to contact the teachers and ask what else I can do at home to help.

Linda Bibee and the Primary Team:

The week before school began we dressed up our classrooms, made lessons plans, and prepared physically and mentally for the weeks to come. On the first day of school, children were escorted to the multi-age/multi-ability homerooms. Some parents accompanied them and questioned us about the placement. "Did our children fail the first year? Is that why they are in the same classroom?" "How is all this going to work out?" The teachers, wearing their best smiles, assured the parents that we had it all under control and that their children were going to get the best education we could manage. What brave words! We were asking ourselves some of those same questions, hoping it would all work out.

The days began. I began to keep a journal of my own. As the children wrote in their journals, my topic was always on the progress of my classroom. I posed questions to myself:

> How can I keep them interested? The first grade children seemed so tired in the afternoon. Being in school for a whole day was a great adjustment for them. The older ones "run over" the younger ones during group discussions. Can I really meet all their needs? Will this all work out?

I kept up a brave front as I plodded through the first weeks of school.

Time in the morning with just seven- and eight-year-olds seemed so familiar. I had moved toward more whole language teaching, and I knew the skills and strengths of the children. I knew their needs and abilities from prior experience. After lunch things changed. The time from 12:30 to 3:00 flew by. It was so different to work with different ages and abilities. We read books together and began to keep an afternoon journal. Of course, some children made pictures in their journals instead of writing words. Other children wrote a few words, maybe completing one or two sentences, and still other children wrote paragraphs. During group participation each child took part. Some of the younger ones had little to say, but we made sure that they felt that everything they said was important.

Jeannie Bass, a Parent:

As the school year began I saw the same pattern of indifference toward school occurring in Alanna. Then one day she came running home. "Mom, guess what we're studying in school?" Before I could answer she replied, "Dinosaurs!" She bubbled on, "Did you know there are several different kinds of dinosaurs? This week we're going to learn about Tyrannosaurs Rex, and next week we're going to study Stegosaurus, and when we're finished studying all of them we get to go to the Natural History Museum!"

What a wonderful change! Since that time her enthusiasm has escalated. Why the change? I believe it's because of the hands-on activities, theme teaching, and whole language approaches our elementary teachers have eagerly adopted.

Linda Bibee and the Primary Team:

We wanted our primary program to be visible. Since we live in a small town, we began to take numerous walking trips through the town. To enhance our study of trees, we walked about the streets and found different kinds of trees. If people were in their yards, we encouraged them to talk with the children about the kinds of trees they had in their yards. My class divided into four groups, and each group adopted a tree in town to study throughout the seasons. What a shame that two of our adopted trees were cut down before the school year ended! In September we studied Johnny Appleseed. We walked a mile through the streets of town so the children could get the feel for walking everywhere as Johnny did. As the leaves of the trees changed, we went leaf collecting. We made booklets with leaves, did leaf rubbings, and made leaf prints with paint. The children read and wrote about the trees every day.

Diana, the Principal:

Traditionally, classes at our school took one or two field trips a year. The primary teachers wanted more field trips. They did a lot of walking about town, as well as visiting museums, downtown Cincinnati, the Cincinnati Zoo, an evergreen farm, a pumpkin patch, and other places. We felt these trips were critical for building the kind of background knowledge necessary for real problem solving, critical thinking, reading, and writing. They encourage hands-on, practical activities and take learning from the classroom into the real world. We welcomed the change in our field trip policies. Enthusiastic, aggressive learners are our goal.

Linda Bibee and the Primary Team:

By October we had really hit our stride in running the multi-age/multi-ability classrooms. Things were settling into a pattern. All children were learning, but we found that the older children craved more details in our studies. As they searched for more complex information, the younger ones, wanting to be like their peers, strived to learn as much as the older ones did. There were no more vocabulary lists consisting of watered-down language. We used authentic vocabulary words, sophisticated words the children chose to learn. We found that during free time and center time, children made smart choices most of the time. They worked and played together well.

As the weeks passed, we knew that the primary team needed more planning time together. We had discovered in the first weeks of school that running a primary program demanded radical changes. It was not feasible to write a curriculum in August and implement the plan throughout the school year without refinement, changes, and even dumping some strategies for new ones. Having a sympathetic administrator who valued our ideas was most helpful. With the aid of our principal, we brainstormed ways to schedule common planning time. Our librarian volunteered to work with the children from 2:00 to 3:00 on Monday, Wednesday, and Friday. Our special needs teacher wanted her children to have physical education with our primary children, so she volunteered to have gym time with the students during the same block of time. In addition, a seventh grade teacher was free from 2:00 to 3:00 each day, and we enlisted her help presenting enrichment topics to children during the week. A rotating schedule with these teachers made it possible for us to have the planning time we needed. The children were participating in worthwhile activities, and we were able to refine our ideas for the ongoing curriculum. Our planning included broad topics and goals for the primary school. We allowed for different teaching styles; we did not mandate specific lesson plans and timetables for all of us to follow.

What is it like to work so closely with another teacher? We became very good friends because we work with one another. Sometimes one person did not like an idea, and it was thrown out. Or we worked through the idea and tried to change it to make everyone happy. Sometimes that did not happen, but in the end all of us felt that we were making the best choices—for ourselves and the children.

Diana, the Principal:

As a school district adapting to transition, Silver Grove's nongraded primary seemed to be meeting the needs and interests of the students. It generated innovative teaching methods from the primary staff and cooperative support personnel. Community members who had expressed concerns prior to the first year have gotten behind the program with enthusiasm. More than 90 percent of the parents and guardians have responded to requests for input/feedback in the form of scheduling parent-teacher conferences or returning survey forms.

Linda Bibee and the Primary Team:

Our first year implementing our primary program ended with a feeling of success, accomplishment, and some questions. Yet we felt that much refinement of the program was still needed. Moving the children from teacher to teacher and room to room in the morning and afternoon made them lose the sense of family and security vital to their success. The teachers found it hard to assign homework, and the children often had to return to their other class to retrieve books or papers they had forgotten. We began to plan for the following school year. We had lots of successes to draw upon and failures to avoid. Since the Kentucky Department of Education now wanted us to include kindergarten in our primary program, we knew we had to revamp our groupings to meet the needs of all the children we were teaching.

Jeannie Bass, a Parent:

By the end of the first year I saw many differences between children in the traditional classroom and those in the flexible classroom environments. For example, April and Amanda, the twins, brought home traditional textbook spelling lists. Alanna brought home spelling words that the children themselves chose from books, experiments, or themes they were working on. The words were usually very challenging, but since the students chose the words, there was more interest in studying and writing the words. I sent the older girls back several times to restudy their spelling words each week. This seldom happened with Alanna because she regularly used her self-chosen spelling words in the many stories and reports she wrote during the class's study of particular themes.

Linda Bibee and the Primary Team:

We began the second year of the primary program with different multi-age groupings. We decided to have self-contained classes of mixed-age children all day. The kindergartners were included with the six- and seven-year-olds for part of the morning.

The start of the school year was much smoother this time. After all, we were dealing with the same children all day. Continuity within the curriculum was apparent. The seven- and eight-year olds had the same teacher as last year. The teachers knew the needs, abilities, and strengths of their children. Except for the students new to our system, the children were accustomed to us, and our "family units" bonded closely.

A typical day in a multi-age/multi-ability classroom at our school begins with free choice time among the students. It is not teacher directed; some children play games not available at other times of the day while others sit and visit with their friends. Surprisingly, by midyear most of the children choose learning activities that they have access to the remainder of the school day. They read and write, solve math problems, and work on the computer. Doing "schoolwork" is an integral part of their lives; learning is important to them.

After the attendance and lunch counts are made, we have calendar time. This is an extended amount of time that encompasses math and language arts activities. We have patterned this calendar time after the Box-It, Bag-It philosophy. For example, for calendar time we asked the children to bring in milk jug lids. We counted these lids, kept a running total of them, and graphed them by color. Other morning activities include the teacher reading books to the children and the children responding to them. We also occasionally teach minilessons to cover strategies for writing or ways to edit.

Later in the morning, children participate in small group reading and literature-response journals. Each day they read silently for an extended period from books they choose. They also work from their writing folders. Some writing topics are teacher inspired, but most are student generated. We want the children to know that they do not have to complete each assignment in one class period and that these assignments can be changed and even thrown out if they become uninteresting to the child.

Our children really like the "Problem of the Day." This is a question posed by the teacher that involves research. Some questions require the use of maps, encyclopedias, dictionaries, or even asking other personnel in the school. The children become very resourceful when looking for the answer to the problem of the day. Examples of posed questions might include, "The president is going to be in Washington State. Where is this and how far away is it?" or, "We have had eight inches of snow this week. When was the last time we had this much snowfall in a week?" The remainder of the morning is spent in center time, with the teacher moving from child to child or group to group facilitating the activities.

In the afternoon we work on our theme unit, which is usually based on science and social studies concepts. We continue to read books aloud to the children, and they read to the class themselves. There is nothing more gratifying than a usually "reluctant-about-reading" child eagerly asking, "Can I read this book to the class?" We end our days with a group analysis of the day's happenings and begin to make plans for the next day and the week to come. Letting the students make choices democratically is important in the multi-age/multi-ability classroom. Empowerment is as important for students as it is for teachers.

Free choice time or center time is most interesting to watch in the multi-age/multi-ability classroom. The children work on many projects. Some read or write stories. Some make up puppet stories with the classroom puppets and puppet stage. Some work on the computer; others work in learning centers counting money in a store situation or telling time. Sometimes a small group will reread a big book, with one child role-playing the teacher. A small number of children, usually the younger ones, still choose play activities. They may be making crude drawings on paper or cutting out crowns for their heads. They may engage in a game of tag within the classroom. The teacher, while recognizing their need for play, eventually tries to direct them to a more structured activity.

The spring of 1993 marked the end of two-and-one-half years of participating in some form of primary school. We have found that we love teaching children in multi-age/multi-ability classrooms. We love the freedom of constructing our own curriculum to meet the needs of the students. We love that the children truly come first within a KERA primary program.

Future plans include expanding the multi-age/multi-ability classroom to five-, six-, seven-, and eight-year-olds in the same classroom for different amounts of time throughout the day. It also includes continuing our development as whole language teachers. We know we will be looking for the best way to teach children by empowering them to learn for themselves.

Jeannie Bass, a Parent:

What I have seen over the past two school years has convinced me that this is a worthwhile program. Even though the twins are succeeding quite well, I can't help wondering how much more they could have accomplished in a holistic program, not just as "good students" but as complete, responsible scholars.

For those parents who say, "The traditional school was good for me. I turned out OK. Why change a good thing?" I want to tell them to look at the many surveys that have been taken. They all say that the United States is falling way behind (not just a little) in education. The cannon and cannonballs were great 100 years ago, too, but would we go into a full-fledged war today with cannons as our heaviest artillery? Our children need to be better educated today than ever.

I support the primary school because it recognizes that children grow and develop as whole people. It emphasizes the social, emotional, and physical well-being all children and respects their individual differences.

Diana, the Principal:

The administrative staff is actively working with the teachers to evaluate and assess the program and its impact on the students. We hope that we are witnessing a new generation of aggressive learners who will adapt their learning practices to gain the most from their educational opportunities.

The constant struggle of a small school to remain self-sufficient and uncompromising in the quality of education it provides can be an inspiration to other small districts to do the same. Silver Grove faculty, staff, and community have always accepted the challenges dealt to us. This is the same strategy we are using in adapting to KERA. We view KERA as a challenge, and we are striving to be constantly and consistently a quality educational system.

Linda Bibee:

I look around my classroom today and ask, "What happened to the students who sat quietly in those neat little rows of desks? What happened to the students who knew better than to ask a neighbor for help with an answer? Those students knew that the teacher was the person in charge!"

I know the answers to my own questions. Those students have been replaced by a new generation of aggressive learners. I'm still "in charge," but in charge of presenting challenges and encouraging investigation rather than answering questions.

Today, students move around my classroom, working in groups, spilling out into the hallway, if necessary, solving problems in creative ways. They talk, help each other, and learn. They question, suggest, and create in ways I could never have imagined when I began teaching twenty-two years ago.

I liked the rows of desks. I liked a quiet room, students bent diligently over their work. Giving that up has not been easy. But eventually, even I could not keep the door closed against new theories in teaching and assessment. Phrases like whole language, holistic grading, and literature-based reading became more commonplace. And unifix cubes sounded innocent enough. I am glad I jumped right in and tried the multi-age/multi-ability classroom. It has made me a better teacher and the children better learners.

Although our school is small, we all agree that we have great hopes and expectations for our children and our school. The children come first!

REFERENCES

Burke D., Snider, A., and Symonds, P. (1980). *Box It or Bag It Mathematics*. Salem, OR: Math Learning Center.

LESSONS ON CREATING NONGRADED PRIMARY PROGRAMS OR IMPLEMENTING OTHER SYSTEMIC CHANGES

BY ELLEN MCINTYRE, RIC A. HOVDA, AND DIANE W. KYLE

CHAPTER

In the past few years, teachers and administrators across the country have responded to calls for educational reforms aimed at enabling more students to become successful learners. In this attempt, educators have implemented many innovative, developmentally appropriate schooling practices. The voices heard in this book express what is needed to implement one of these innovations—nongraded primary programs. What are the lessons? What can we learn about primary programs specifically? This chapter summarizes the experiences of the teachers and administrators in this book and highlights the important themes that emerged.

▓ LESSONS ON CREATING NONGRADED PROGRAMS

According to the teachers and principals featured in this book, change is gradual and must be met with patience and humor. They also insist that it takes many people to bring about successful systemic change. And they convey that understanding children and learning leads to good classroom practices. Let's examine each of these lessons.

"Times they are a-changin' . . .*".* Teachers have historically been asked to do it all—be experts in every subject area and "go it alone" with twenty-five or more children. But, thankfully, times are changing.

One major change is an increase in professional collaboration. Recall the example of Tina, Joy, and Donna from Atkinson Elementary team teaching a lesson on insects. Donna directly taught a short lesson to the entire class while Joy monitored the group and Tina took anecdotal records. Later they divided the class into three smaller groups for more specific lessons. Phil and Cheryl from Wilt Elementary demonstrated the same kind of teaching, ensuring that the children with special needs understood the concepts and participated in the lessons. Even when teachers cannot teach together, they can plan together, as all the teachers featured in this book described. Teachers can combine resources to learn from each other. They can learn to "share instead of hoard," as Anne and Geraldine from Spencer County Elementary taught us. Now, more than ever, teachers use the strengths of a wide variety of people. Sharing human and material resources is necessary and productive for change.

The teachers in this book share the view that children are the best informants on what to change in the classroom and how to change it. Katherine from Chenoweth Elementary began to change when she truly considered what the *children* wanted. She thought about what she had wanted and responded to as a child and found her students to be much like herself—they wanted active, meaningful, and functional tasks and projects. Similarly, the teachers at LaGrange and Saffel Street schools carefully examined children's work for evidence of what children needed and wanted. Bridget and Lisa at Ward Chapel Elementary, after alternating between active, thematic teaching and traditional worksheet activities, observed the differences in children's responses. Needless to say, the children showed them that the thematic approach was much better! Beverly from Squires Elementary also carefully questioned what she was doing and how the children were responding. She continually observed her children as they worked and asked herself, "Are the children learning what they need to be learning? What else do they need to know?" All teachers agreed that the most effective way to know what to change is to observe carefully children's actions and work. Questions like, "Are the children actively engaged?" "Do they seem happy?" and, "What else do they need to learn?" can help teachers focus on creating child-centered classrooms.

Change occurs gradually. Many of the teachers and principals described the decisions they made and how they later learned that some of their decisions were not the best but were still a natural part of change. They learned to laugh at their trials and be patient with themselves. "Change is evolutionary," concluded Anne and Geraldine from Spencer County Elementary, and "learning to be a team partner is a journey." At Ward Chapel and Millard schools, teachers who teamed had not only different personalities but, at least at the beginning, also very different theoretical perspectives on teaching and learning. Because they had respect for each other and were open to change, they gradually learned how to team together, and their philosophies became more alike. Remember Cold Spring Elementary's Cathy Cool's "rule" for change? "People change at their own speed, in their own way, and when they are ready." Patience, respect, and humor seem to be the keys.

In summary, among the lessons learned about change are that change is easier if educators collaborate with one another, and the best way to know how and what to change about instruction is to observe and respond to the children. Finally, all educators can come to accept that change occurs gradually.

It takes a whole village to raise a child." The truth of this now-famous African proverb becomes more and more clear in creating primary programs. Joe, the principal of Camden Station Elementary, stressed the importance of "bringing in all the stakeholders" when implementing systemic change. In his school, the stakeholders in the primary program include the school counselor, the cafeteria workers, the custodian, the business community, and parents, as well as the teachers and children. In some way, each of these people had a direct impact on what children in his school learned.

Certainly it helps when parents are involved with the schools. Activities such as "Math Nights" at Camden Station Elementary, in which parents actually participated in the kinds of activities their children do, can be instrumental in helping parents understand the change. Better and more frequent communication has occurred in many of the schools. At LaGrange Elementary, the teachers worked hard to determine the best ways to report to parents how their children were progressing.

They too held many family meetings in the evenings. Parents can also be the biggest advocates of the primary program, once they understand it. At Silver Grove Elementary, one parent said about her daughter and her classmates, "They have more opportunity to learn than ever before."

Bringing in all the "stakeholders" enables classrooms to obtain the sense of community so apparent in many of the teachers' classrooms. Children can learn to see many different people in the school as part of the "family." In Katherine's classroom, the children learned to support each other, help each other, and even protect each other in the way families often do. Donna, Joy, and Tina from Atkinson Elementary and Karen from Millard Elementary agreed that the first day of school during the second year of the primary program felt "less like a first day and more like a reunion."

Understanding children and learning. The teachers featured in this book had one thing in common—the desire to understand children and meet students' needs in the best ways possible. They obtained information in a variety of ways. Some read professional books on development and teaching, such as Regie Routman's *Invitations*, Wiggington's *Sometimes a Shining Moment*, Dewey's *Experience and Education*, and others. Others attended workshops and institutes on whole language, writing process, or hands-on mathematics. They all came to the same conclusions about appropriate settings and instructional practices. Below is a list of the common practices and attributes of these classrooms:

- warm, caring atmosphere
- respect for children
- careful observations of children
- daily read-aloud time
- extensive self-directed learning time (i.e., learning centers, reading and writing "workshops")
- active, hands-on activities (e.g., using manipulatives for mathematics)
- large blocks of time for intensive study
- thematic teaching

- reading literature and writing for authentic purposes
- music and art a natural part of the day
- attention to each "critical attribute" of the primary program

Each of these classrooms needed time to become fully developmentally appropriate. None of the teachers made huge leaps at one time but instead took many small steps. Bridget and Lisa at Ward Chapel described their first steps toward developmentally appropriate practices. They began simply by reading more to the children. Then they began to incorporate more silent reading time, and they invited the children to write and share entries in their daily journals. Other classrooms might begin with increasing parent involvement or just watching and thinking about the children. Small steps each month or each year will result in major changes overall. Again, change takes time, patience, and humor.

Understanding *all* children is critical to the success of the primary program, because children with learning disabilities and special gifts are now expected to spend all or most of their time in the general program. Phil and Cheryl from Wilt Elementary and Tina, Joy, and Donna from Atkinson Elementary showed the positive impact nongraded classrooms have on children with learning disabilities and other special needs. In particular, Phil and Cheryl detailed how children with multiple handicaps exhibited what they knew in less-traditional ways. The teachers at LaGrange show how they assess and build on children's artistic gifts. All the teachers allow advanced readers and writers to choose their own texts to read, write, and share. These teachers embraced the concept of continuous progress—the view that *all* children have particular interests, capabilities, strengths, and needs. They provided instruction to meet those needs and celebrated children's strengths, whatever they happened to be.

■ SYSTEMIC CHANGE: LESSONS FOR PROFESSIONAL DEVELOPMENT

What do the experiences of teachers, principals, and parents tell us about what they need most when making educational change? The answers were overwhelmingly the same: intense professional development experiences, support, and time.

Professional Development. Foxfire. Summer Writing Project. Whole language and *Math Their Way* workshops. National Alliance for Restructuring. Project Discovery. Personal and professional writing. Graduate courses. Research. These are the kinds of professional development experiences the teachers and principals featured in this book found most helpful in making real change. They were long-term, in-depth experiences that enabled the teachers to change their *thinking* about teaching and learning. What seems to be a major part of these experiences is a focus on children's development and the most appropriate purposeful activity that meets their needs. The teachers learned about *people* (children and themselves) and how they best learn, which enabled them to make good choices in the classrooms. They were experiences designed to change teachers' thinking and actions.

The teachers featured in this book read professional books and talked with colleagues about those readings. They spent time reflecting (and even writing) about their practices. Some teachers, like those at Mason-Corinth Elementary, invited experts into their school to critique them and make suggestions. Others visited neighboring schools to observe, and all continually sought to improve their practices.

All educators need intensive experiences aimed at fostering reflection and learning, as change follows from learning. They also need time to talk with colleagues about their changing views. These are also the kinds of experiences needed in university teacher-education programs. University courses need to be models for developmentally appropriate practices, authentic assessment, and collaboration, very similar to what is expected of teachers.

Support. Support for change can come from many different groups or people and in many different ways. The chapters by the teachers at Silver Grove, Mason-Corinth, LaGrange, and Camden Station schools describe how the principals provided extensive support to their primary teachers. The principals provided resources teachers needed, rearranged schedules so teachers had planning time together, and stayed out of teachers' ways. Mason-Corinth teachers said their principal gave them "freedom to experiment without constraint." The assistant principal even took over classes from time to time in order to give teachers common planning time. Diana, the principal from Silver Grove, agreed that this was necessary and said, "The key to success of the primary program is empowerment of teachers." Time to learn and experiment in collaboration with others is most helpful.

Teachers also need support from each other. They need opportunities to see each other teach and to reflect on their practices. At Atkinson, the teachers had the opportunity to take different instructional roles as they guided and monitored student learning because the three teachers shared one classroom. Karen, from Millard Elementary, who also had this opportunity during her second year of the primary programs said, "I found that working as a team meant making adjustments. . . ." Indeed, teaming does take adjusting, but it can also be rewarding. Anne and Geraldine from Spencer County Elementary claimed that it "takes some pressure off when you know another professional is working on solving the same problems." They also began talking to other colleagues in their building to learn from them. However it is done, it helps when teachers know they no longer have to "go it alone." Support for and from each other is one step in making large-scale change reasonable and attainable.

"Time!" "Time!" is the response heard often when teachers are asked what they need most to implement their primary program successfully. They want time to learn about children and teaching and time to read the great educational books that have been recently published. Teachers want time to plan new units and lessons with other teachers. They want time to *observe* other teachers in action. They want time to meet with other teachers to talk about the particular characteristics of the children they share, their needs and wants. They want time to reflect and write about their practice. They want time with the children themselves—to observe them and talk to them. And as the principal of Camden Station said, teachers and administrators "need time to let KERA take effect."

In order for teachers to truly become professionals, they need school-sanctioned time to act as professionals. Teachers can discuss research and the best practices that support learning. They can share ideas and resources. They can divide work to become more efficient.

They can talk about particular needs of children and solve problems together. But they must be allowed some time during the school day to do this.

■ CONCLUSION

When Anne and Geraldine from Spencer County Elementary stepped back and examined their struggles and the radical changes they had accomplished, they realized (with some exasperation!) that they had only taken "two baby steps on what seemed like an endless journey." Indeed, all the teachers and principals recognized that continual change is necessary. As the teachers from Mason-Corinth put it, educators must "keep reaching for the stars" in order to understand the ever-changing groups of children and their needs. With continual change come new challenges, but also the promise of better teaching and more effective learning. Ultimately, how to provide a brighter future for young children is the most important lesson we can learn.

REFERENCES

Barath, Corton (1976). *Mathematics Their Way*. Menlo Park, CA: Addison-Wesley.

Dewey, J. (1938). *Experience and Education*. NY: Collier Books.

Routman, R. (1991). *Invitations*. Portsmouth, NH: Heinemann.

Wigginton, E. (1986). *Sometimes a Shining Moment*. Garden City, NY: Anchor Books.

PROFESSIONAL DEVELOPMENT POSSIBILITIES

BY RIC A. HOVDA, DIANE W. KYLE, AND ELLEN MCINTYRE

CHAPTER 16

As the roles of principals and teachers change in restructured schools, so must the professional development provided to support them. The traditional in-service model of bringing in an "outside" expert for a three-hour presentation cannot address the complex issues educators face or provide the sustained support necessary for lasting change. In restructured schools, much of the professional development occurs in planned, ongoing programs, intensive institutes, and school-based study groups. The teachers represented in our case studies report that they have been involved in extensive professional development over the past few years to prepare them for primary classrooms. The most helpful professional development, teachers suggest, is interactive and reflective. Below we suggest professional development ideas appropriate for the cases presented in this book—ideas that promote interaction and reflection.

Ideas Across Chapters. The following activities can be used with any of the chapters.

1. *Easy/Hard.* Primary schools in Kentucky are developed around seven "critical attributes." List these critical attributes and ask individuals to put an *E* for easy and an *H* for hard beside each attribute and explain why it would be easy or hard to implement. Gather in small groups to compare

responses and discuss reasons for similarities and differences in them. The small groups can then report back to the whole group. What factors seem to promote/inhibit development of these attributes?

This activity can focus on either the participants' own teaching situations or the collection of cases presented in the book.

2. *Take a Stand.* Ask each participant to write on a sheet of paper a statement of belief about a specified topic. In small groups, have one person place her or his statement in the middle of a table. Each participant should consider the statement and then place a 3" × 5" card near the statement to the degree to which she or he agrees with it and explain the placement. For example, on the topic of multi-age/multi-ability grouping the statement might read:

THE OPTIMUM AGE RANGE
IN A MULTI-AGE/MULTI-ABILITY
CLASSROOM IS TWO YEARS.

The person placing the statement explains it by sharing the knowledge base and personal experience that supports it. A participant who agrees with the statement places his or her card over the statement and further develops the rationale. Participants who have other perspectives place their cards in proximity of agreement with the statement and explain the placement.

This activity promotes lively discussion and debate. The purpose is not to bring the group to consensus but rather to clarify and refine beliefs by seeing multiple perspectives on issues.

3. *Jigsaw.* Assign individual chapters of this book to small groups (or individuals). Each group reads the assigned chapter and discusses a set of questions posed by the group. Questions might include the following:

What lessons about change were learned?

What did teachers report as the most challenging aspects of implementing primary schools?

What suggestions did teachers make about implementing multi-age/multi-ability classrooms?

4. *Critical Attributes.* Seven "critical attributes" characterize Kentucky's primary program. As you survey the chapters, what lessons about their implementation have the most applicability to your own setting? How might you modify what has been done to better suit your school? What kinds of professional development might be necessary for further growth?

■ DISCUSSION QUESTIONS/IDEAS FOR INDIVIDUAL CHAPTERS

Chapter 2 (Chenoweth School)

■ Teacher Katherine Alexander shares her daily schedule by relating personal beliefs that guide each time block. Outline your own daily schedule, sharing the beliefs that guide each time block.

■ Many teachers subscribe to the belief that "teachers teach who they are." Do you subscribe to this belief? Why? What are the implications of your belief for professional development of educators?

■ Katherine Alexander shares milestones in her professional development and describes how these milestones influenced her present practices. Create a timeline of milestones in your own career. Share these with a colleague and discuss what you project as a next step in your professional development.

■ Ms. Alexander's classroom is organized around the idea that children's learning is their work and thus they work out of "offices." What other elements of a "work culture" are evident in her classroom? What orientation would best characterize your classroom culture? School culture? Give examples.

Chapter 3 (Spencer County School)

■ Elementary teaching has traditionally been an isolated profession. Thus, forming teaching teams presents challenges to the professional culture of elementary teaching (as Anne and Geraldine from Taylorsville School describe). What experiences in pre-professional teacher education would you suggest to prepare teachers for such work? What skills and attitudes are required to be effective team members? How should practicing teachers prepare themselves to become successful team members?

■ What changes in current traditional elementary school practices and procedures must be addressed if teachers are to work in teams?

■ What are the advantages to having teacher teams in primary schools? What are the disadvantages? Do the advantages outweigh the disadvantages? Why? How do you feel Anne and Geraldine would respond to these questions?

■ How has teaming worked for you? What were your struggles?

Chapter 4 (Cold Spring School)

■ Cathy Cool suggests five rules that she has developed from her experience with implementing a primary program. Discuss these rules and consider how they reflect your own experiences with educational change. What "rules" have you developed?

■ *Stop, Look, and Listen* is a strategy teacher Cathy Cool uses to reflect on her teaching. Describe a recent time when you used this type of approach and discuss what you learned from the experience.

Chapter 5 (LaGrange School)

■ The teachers from LaGrange School share several examples of methods/instruments they use for authentic assessment. What do these approaches tell us about student progress that more traditional approaches do not? On the other hand, what do more traditional assessments reveal about student progress that authentic assessments do not? Are the two approaches theoretically compatible? Why? Why not?

■ The teachers from LaGrange School talk about "making sense" of anecdotal notes. How do the teachers make sense of anecdotal notes? What are the frames of reference for such information?

■ Authentic assessment is a growing movement in education. What must teachers learn in order to productively use this approach to assessment? What assumptions about the role of assessment in instruction are made in using authentic assessment?

■ Changing assessment strategies requires new perspectives for parents as well. How are teachers at LaGrange School addressing this issue? What other suggestions might help parents understand the value of authentic assessment?

Chapter 6 (Atkinson School)

Atkinson School's program represents a wide range in the ages and abilities of students.

■ What kinds of collaboration occur among children of varied ages and abilities? How do they learn from each other?

What do the three teachers gain from teaching the same group of children? What do the children gain?

What are some ways children benefit by having the same teachers for three or four years? What might be some disadvantages?

Chapter 7 (Paxton Wilt School)

■ Teachers Philip Poore and Cheryl Armstrong suggest that full inclusion of special needs learners is possible because of their multi-age, continuous progress model. What features of their program promote a successful inclusion model? How does a multi-age program facilitate inclusion? How feasible is full inclusion in a graded, sequential-skills program?

■ What beliefs about special needs learners do Poore and Armstrong hold? What beliefs are necessary for a full inclusion model to be successful?

Chapter 8 (Saffell Street School)

■ Consider the contents of the portfolios kept by the teachers at Saffell Street School. What can these items show that more traditional assessments cannot?

■ What assumptions about assessment are made by advocates of authentic assessment? How do these assumptions impact instruction?

■ What implied benefits of authentic assessment do the teachers at Saffell Street School discuss? How do these benefits relate to your assessment concerns?

Chapter 9 (Ward Chapel School)

■ The Ward Chapel teachers describe how they implemented each of the seven critical attributes of Kentucky's primary schools. What lessons do these descriptions teach us about mandated, top-down change?

■ If your school were to use the seven critical attributes as a framework for developing your primary unit, how would you initially assess your present program on a scale of one (low level of implementation) to five (high level of implementation)? Discuss your ratings with colleagues.

■ How do the seven critical attributes adopted by Kentucky match your knowledge of the literature on and your experience with primary education? Which attributes would you alter/refine to meet your particular orientation to primary education? What attributes might you add?

■ If you were just beginning a nongraded primary program, which of the attributes would you suggest as the most effective starting point? Why?

Chapter 10 (Millard School)

■ Many teachers can name a "defining moment" in their professional development. Teacher Karen Adkins suggests that her participation in Foxfire was a defining moment for her. What do you see as your defining moment as a professional? Are there any common attributes/characteristics of defining moments among your colleagues?

Chapter 11 (Squires School)

■ Like many teachers, Beverly Wells questioned herself about teaching "skills." She describes her journey in confronting the issue in her own teaching. Share your perspective about issues related to teaching skills in early childhood programs. What advice do you have for other teachers about this issue?

Chapter 12 (Mason-Corinth School)

■ What advice could teachers give to new principals about facilitating change?

■ What qualities are the most important in considering candidates for a leadership position in schools in the process of restructuring?

■ Planning time is often mentioned as a critical need for teachers. Brainstorm at least five ways to provide planning time and be specific about the changes necessary to provide the time.

Chapter 13 (Camden Station School)

■ Principal Joe Jacovino states, "Massive change can cause massive stress." List several of the stresses he describes and also any strategies his school used to address stress. Do you notice any common features of these strategies? What might they suggest for future strategies?

■ What can we learn from Camden Station School about systemic educational reform?

Chapter 14 (Silver Grove School)

■ Forming partnerships between parents, administrators, and teachers is challenging. What do you see as the important links to forming partnerships at Silver Grove School? From your experience, what are critical features of successful educational partnerships?

■ Silver Grove School promotes student empowerment through choice. What opportunities for choice do you feel are important for young children?

■ In forming teams, many primary schools initially chose to adopt a departmentalized approach. Discuss the challenges a departmentalized approach presents when a school is implementing an integrated, thematic and continuous progress curriculum.

BIBLIOGRAPHY

PUBLICATIONS ON NONGRADED SETTINGS AND RELATED TOPICS:

Anderson, R. H., & Pavan, B. N. (1993). *Nongradedness: Helping it to happen.* Lancaster, PA: Technomics Publishing.

Baskwill, J. (1989). *Parents and teachers. Partners in learning.* Richmond Hill, Ontario: Scholastic Canada.

Braddock, J. H. II, & McPartland, J. M. (April 1990). Alternatives to tracking. *Educational Leadership,* 76–80.

Bredekamp, S. (Ed.). (1987). *Developmentally appropriate practice in early childhood programs serving children from birth through age 8,* expanded ed. Washington, DC: National Association for the Education of Young Children.

Cushman, K. (Summer 1990). The whys and hows of the multi-age primary classroom. *American Educator,* 28–39.

Gutiérrez, R., & Slavin, R. E. (Winter 1992). Achievement effects of the nongraded elementary school: A best evidence synthesis. *Review of Educational Research, 62,* 333–76.

Henderson, A. T. (October 1988). Parents are a school's best friend. *Phi Delta Kappan,* 149–53.

Pavan, B. N. (1992). School effectiveness and nongraded schools. Paper presented at the Annual Meeting of the American Educational Research Association, San Francisco.

The Prichard Committee for Academic Excellence (July 1992). Primary school, school-based decision making, family resource/youth services centers. First Year Reports to the Prichard Committee at its July 1992 Annual Meeting.

Slavin, R. E. (September 1988). Synthesis of research on grouping in elementary and secondary schools. *Educational Leadership,* 67–77.

State Regulations and Recommended Best Practices for Kentucky's Primary Program (January 1993). Frankfort, KY: Kentucky Department of Education.

White, C. (1990). *Jevon doesn't sit at the back anymore.* New York: Scholastic.

■ BOOKS TO HELP WITH INTEGRATED INSTRUCTION:

Balding, G., & Richards, N. (1990). *Springboards: Ideas for science.* Albany, NY: Delmar Publishers.

Butzlow, C. M., & Butzlow, J. W. (1989). *Science through children's literature.* Englewood, CO: Teacher Ideas Press.

Cerbus, D. P., & Rice, C. F. (1991). *Connecting science and literature.* Westminster, CA: Teacher Created Materials.

Charlesworth, R., & Lind, K. K. (1990). *Math and science for young children.* Albany, NY: Delmar Publishers.

Cochran, J. (1992). *Integrating science and literature.* New York: Incentive.

Dori, E. (1991). *Doing what scientists do.* Portsmouth, NH: Heinemann.

Fredericks, A. D. (1991). *Social studies through children's literature.* Englewood, CO: Libraries Unlimited (division of Teacher Ideas Press).

Harlan, J. (1988). *Science experiences for early childhood.* New York: Macmillan.

Harlen, W. (1988). *Primary science: Taking the plunge.* Portsmouth, NH: Heinemann.

Laughlin, M., et al. (1991). *Social studies readers' theater for children—scripts and script development.* Englewood, CO: Teacher Ideas Press.

Marcuccio, P. R. (1990). *Science and children.* Washington, DC: National Science Teachers Association.

Natoli, S. J. (Ed.). *Social education.* Washington, DC: National Council for the Social Studies.

Richards, N. (1990). *Springboards: Ideas for social studies.* Albany, NY: Delmar Publishers.

Saul, W., & Jagusch, S. A. (1991). *Vital connections—children, science, and books.* Portsmouth, NH: Heinemann.

Thompson, G. (1991). *Teaching through themes.* New York: Scholastic.

Walsh, H. M. *Social studies and the young learner.* Washington, DC: National Council for the Social Studies.

Wiggington, E. (February 1989). Foxfire grows up. *Harvard Educational Review,* 24–49.

▨ BOOKS TO HELP WITH LITERACY TEACHING:

Allen, J., & Mason, J.M. (Eds.). (1989). *Risk takers, risk breakers: Reducing the risks for young literacy learners.* Portsmouth, NH: Heinemann.

Baghban, M. (1989). *You can help your young child with writing.* Newark, DE: International Reading Association.

Barron, M. (1990). *I learn to read and write the way I learn to talk.* Katonah, NY: Richard C. Owen.

Barrs, M., Ellis, S., Tester, H., & Thomas, A. (1989). *The primary language record: Handbook for teachers.* Portsmouth, NH: Heinemann.

Baskwill, J., & Whitman, P. (1988). *Evaluation: Whole language, whole child.* New York: Scholastic.

Batzle, J. (1992). *Portfolio assessment and evaluation—developing and using portfolios in the K–6 classroom.* Cypress, CA: Creative Teaching Press.

Bauer, K., & Drew, R. (1992). *Alternatives to worksheets: Motivational reading and writing activities across the curriculum.* Cypress, CA: Creative Teaching Press.

Bird, L. B. (Ed.). (1989). *Becoming a whole language school: The Fair Oaks story.* Katonah, NY: Richard C. Owen.

Bissex, G. L., & Bullock, R. (Eds.). (1987). *Seeing for ourselves: Case-study research by teachers of writing.* Portsmouth, NH: Heinemann.

Bruner, J., & Cole, M. (1990). *Early literacy. The developing child.* Cambridge: Harvard University Press.

Burchby, M. (Spring 1988). Literature and whole language. *The New Advocate,* 114–23.

Butler, D., & Clay, M. (1987, 1988). *Reading begins at home. Writing begins at home.* Portsmouth, NH: Heinemann.

Cambourne, B. (1988). *The whole story: Natural learning and the acquisition of literacy in the classroom.* Richmond Hill, Ontario: Scholastic—TAB.

Cudd, E. T., & Roberts, L. (February 1989). Using writing to enhance content area learning in the primary grades. *The Reading Teacher,* 392–404.

Cullinan, B. E. (1989). *Literature and the child,* 2d ed. San Diego: Harcourt Brace Jovanovich.

Cutting, B. (1990). *Getting started in whole language.* Bothell, WA: The Wright Group.

Doake, D. B. (1988). *Reading begins at birth*. New York: Scholastic.

Eisele, B. (1991). *Managing the whole language classroom—A complete teaching resource guide for K–6 teachers*. Cypress, CA: Creative Teaching Press.

Fisher, B. (1991). *Joyful learning: A whole language kindergarten*. Portsmouth, NH: Heinemann.

Gibson, L. (1989). *Literacy learning in the early years: Through children's eyes*. New York: Teachers College Press.

Goodman, K., Goodman, Y., & Hood, W. (Eds.) (1989). *The whole language evaluation book*. Portsmouth, NH: Heinemann.

Hancock, J., & Hill, S. (Eds.). (1987). *Literature-based reading programs at work*. Portsmouth, NH: Heinemann.

Heald-Taylor, G. (1989). *The administrator's guide to whole language*. Katonah, NY: Richard C. Owen.

Hearne, B. (1990). *Choosing books for children. A common sense guide*, revised and expanded ed. New York: Delacorte.

Heltshe, M. A., & Kirchner, A. B. (1991). *Multicultural explorations: Joyous journeys with books*. Englewood, CO: Teacher Ideas Press.

Hickman, J., & Cullinan, B. E. (Eds.) (1989). *Children's literature in the classroom: Weaving Charlotte's Web*. Norwood, MA: Christopher-Gordon. (hardbound)

Hill, M. W. (1989). *Home: Where reading and writing begin*. Portsmouth, NH: Heinemann.

Hornsby, D., & Sukarna, D. (1988). *Read on—a conference approach to reading*. Portsmouth, NH: Heinemann.

Karelitz, E. B. (1993). *The author's chair and beyond: Language and literacy in a primary classroom*. Portsmouth, NH: Heinemann.

Korbrin, B. (1988). *Eyeopeners! How to choose and use children's books about real people, places, and things*. New York: Penguin.

Lipson, E. R. (1988). *The New York Times parent's guide to the best books for children*. New York: Random House.

McIntyre, E., & Pressley, M. (1996). *Balanced instruction: Strategies and skills in whole language*. Norwood, NJ: Christopher-Gordon Press.

Mills, H., & Clyde, J. A. (Eds.) (1990). *Portraits of whole language classrooms: Learning for all ages*. Portsmouth, NH: Heinemann.

Moen, C. B. (1991). *Teaching with Caldecott books: Activities across the curriculum.* New York: Scholastic.

Moir, H., Cain, M., & Prosak-Beres, L. (Eds.) (1990). *Collected perspectives: Choosing and using books for the classroom.* Norwood, MA: Christopher-Gordon.

Mooney, M. E. (1990). *Reading to, with, and by children.* Katonah, NY: Richard C. Owen.

Morrow, L. M. (1989). *Literacy development in the early years.* Englewood Cliffs, NJ: Prentice Hall.

Newkirk, T. (1989). *More than stories: The range of children's writing.* Portsmouth, NH: Heinemann.

O'Berry, L. (1993). *Storytime around the curriculum: A comprehensive early childhood curriculum presented through literature.* New York: Partner Press (Gyphon House).

Pace, G. (March 1992). Stories of teacher-initiated change from traditional to whole-language literacy instruction. *The Elementary School Journal, 92,* 461–76.

Pappas, C. C., Kiefer, B. Z., & Levstik, L. S. (1990). *An integrated language perspective in the elementary school: Theory into action.* White Plains, NY: Longman.

Parry, J. A., & Hornsby, D. (1985). *Write on! A conference approach to writing.* Portsmouth, NH: Heinemann.

Rhodes, L. K., & Dudley-Marling, C. (1988). *Readers and writers with a difference: A holistic approach to teaching learning disabled and remedial students.* Portsmouth, NH: Heinemann.

Routman, R. (1991). *Invitations.* Portsmouth, NH: Heinemann.

Routman, R. (1988). *Transitions: From literature to literacy.* Portsmouth, NH: Heinemann.

Rudman, M. K. (1989). *Children's literature: Resources for the classroom.* Norwood, MA: Christopher-Gordon.

Short, K., & Pierce, K. M. (Eds.) (1990). *Talking about books: Creating literature communities.* Portsmouth, NH: Heinemann.

Stillman, P. (1989). *Families writing.* Cincinnati, OH: Writer's Digest Books. Portsmouth, NH: Heinemann.

Strickland, D. S., & Morrow, L. M. (Eds.) (1989). *Emerging literacy: Young children learn to read and write.* Newark, DE: International Reading Association.

Taylor, D., & Dorsey-Gaines, C. (1988). *Growing up literate: Learning from inner-city families*. Portsmouth, NH: Heinemann.

Tierney, R. J., Carter, M. A., & Desai, L. E. (1991). *Portfolios in the reading-writing classroom*. Norwood, MA: Christopher-Gordon.

Tompkins, G., & McGee, L. (1993). *Teaching reading with literature, case studies to action plans*. New York: Macmillan.

Topping, K. (March 1989). Peer tutoring and paired reading: Combining two powerful techniques. *The Reading Teacher*, 488–94.

Trelease, J. (1990). *The new read-aloud handbook*. New York: Penguin.

Watson, D., Burke, C., & Harste, J. (1989). *Whole language: Inquiring voices*. Richmond Hill, Ontario: Scholastic—TAB.

Weaver, C. (1990). *Understanding whole language: From principles to practice*. Portsmouth, NH: Heinemann.

■ BOOKS TO HELP WITH MATHEMATICS TEACHING:

Abrohms, A. (1992). *Literature-based math activities—an integrated approach*. New York: Scholastic Books.

Baker, A., & Baker, J. (1990). *Mathematics in process*. Portsmouth, NH: Heinemann.

Burns, M. (1992). *About teaching math: A K–8 resource guide*. Math Solutions Publications.

Burns, M. (1992). *Math and literature (K–3)*. Math Solutions Publications.

Carratello, J., & Carratello, P. (1992). *Connecting math and literature*. Teacher Created Materials.

Charles, L. H., & Brummett, M. R. (1989). *Connections: Linking manipulatives to mathematics (grades 1–6)*. Sunnyvale, CA: Creative Publications.

Griffiths, R., & Clyne, M. (1990). *Books you can count on: Linking mathematics and literature*. Albany, NY: Delmar Publishers.

Rommel, C. A. (1991). *Integrating beginning math and literature*. Incentive Publishers.

Van de walle, J. (1994). *Elementary school math*. New York: Longman.

Whitin, D. J., Mills, H., & O'Keefe, T. (1990). *Living and learning mathematics: Stories and strategies for supporting mathematical literacy*. Portsmouth, NH: Heinemann.

Whitin, D., & Wilde, S. (1992). *Read any good math lately? Children's books for mathematical learning, K–6*. Portsmouth, NH: Heinemann.

INDEX